OUR BLACK SONS MATTER

OUR BLACK SONS MATTER

Mothers Talk about Fears, Sorrows, and Hopes

Edited by George Yancy, Maria del Guadalupe Davidson, and Susan Hadley

ROWMAN & LITTLEFIELD
Lanham • Boulder • New York • London

Published by Rowman & Littlefield
A wholly owned subsidiary of
The Rowman & Littlefield Publishing Group, Inc.
4501 Forbes Boulevard, Suite 200, Lanham, Maryland 20706
https://rowman.com

Unit A, Whitacre Mews, 26-34 Stannary Street, London SE11 4AB,
United Kingdom

British Library Cataloguing in Publication Information Available

Library of Congress Cataloging-in-Publication Data
Names: Yancy, George, editor of compilation. | Davidson, Maria del Guada-
    lupe, editor of compilation. | Hadley, Susan (Susan Joan), 1967- editor of
    compilation.
Title: Our black sons matter : mothers talk about fears, sorrows, and hopes /
    edited by George Yancy, Maria del Guadalupe Davidson, and Susan Had-
    ley.
Other titles: Mothers talk about fears, sorrows, and hopes
Description: Lanham, MD : Rowman & Littlefield, [2016] | Includes biblio-
    graphical references and index.
Identifiers: LCCN 2016023174 (print) | LCCN 2016025477 (ebook) | ISBN
    9781442269118 (cloth : alk. paper) | ISBN 9781442269125 (electronic)
Subjects: LCSH: African American young men. | African American boys. |
    Mothers and sons—United States. | African Americans—Family relation-
    ships.
Classification: LCC E185.86 .O85 2016 (print) | LCC E185.86 (ebook) | DDC
    305.242/108896073—dc23
LC record available at http://lccn.loc.gov/2016023174

∞ ™ The paper used in this publication meets the minimum requirements of
American National Standard for Information Sciences Permanence of Paper
for Printed Library Materials, ANSI/NISO Z39.48-1992.

Printed in the United States of America

I dedicate this book to all Black bodies that have been, that are presently being, and that will be hurt, violated, and killed by racial and racist injustice. By extension, this book is dedicated to all human beings. Our bodies are fragile and can be wounded through violence. Yet, these same fragile bodies expose us to the touch of love, care, and gentleness. May we learn how to respect and care for our mutual fragility, vulnerability, and exposure.

—George Yancy

This book is dedicated to my mother Florence Leonora Morris Edwards (1930–2015) and my dear friend Jonathan M. Fabian (1973–2016).

—Maria del Guadalupe Davidson

To all mothers of Black children living in the mire of a white supremacist world. May Martin Luther King, Jr.'s dream one day become a reality. And to my four wonderful Black sons—I love you.

—Susan Hadley

CONTENTS

ACKNOWLEDGMENTS

George Yancy: The contributors are to be thanked for their tenacity, audacity, and love for addressing a very serious problem in twenty-first century North America, a problem that has haunted Black bodies since their tortuous journey through the middle passage. And while all Black bodies didn't arrive here through the same route, they have come to understand and to bear the weight of being Black in relation to the oppressive structures of white supremacy and the insidious operations of whiteness. We are all in this deep political, social, affective mess together. We will rise as one or fall together. My hope is that it will be the former. My mother and father are to be thanked for giving birth to a precious Black boy. Your spirit and flesh will continue to live through me. Though my sons are loved beyond words, I will continue to speak them. Know that the lived experience of being raced is only one aspect of who you are. You are also a deep mystery, a multiplicity, a moment of consciousness within a cosmos of which we have understood only a fraction. I wish that I could tell you in unambiguous terms why you are here, but I can't. I do hope, though, that this universe and your moment of consciousness means more than the meaning that you/we create. Your dad is a hopeful theist. He will remain so to the grave. This is to say that I regard our being here as an incredible event, one that has divine significance. Given this, what we do between birth and the grave is our moment. Don't allow your Black bodies to be torn asunder by those who would rather you didn't exist. You are loved by me, your mother, and ancestors from both lines of descent. And if what I think/ feel (hope for) is true, you are loved by a deeper mystery that I don't pretend to be able to understand. To Susan, thanks for being my partner in the loving guidance that we have shown and continue to show our sons. Thanks for understanding the complexity of what it means to exist as Black. And thanks for your maternal love, and its beautiful simplicity.

Maria del Guadalupe Davidson: I want to thank my friends and colleagues at the University of Oklahoma, especially Dr. Kirsten Edwards, Dr. Merelsie (Melli) Velazquez, Dr. Elon Dancy, Dr. Catherine John, Dr. Clemencia Rodriguez, Dr. Roxanne Mountford, and Dr. Roksana Alavi for making safe places, for their fearlessness, and for their never-ending pursuit of racial and gender justice. Finally, even as we fight to protect our black sons, we must never forget that our black daughters need to be protected as well. Black Girls' Lives Matter.

Susan Hadley: I would like to thank all of the contributors in this volume for sharing the vulnerabilities of motherhood that are nuanced by a racialized world. Your strength and love is a continual inspiration. I would like to thank my co-editors for their collegiality and mutual commitment to social justice and love for Black children. To my parents, thank you for instilling in me a sense of social justice. To my mother-in-law, sister-in-law, and niece-in-law, you have been a wonderful source of knowledge and strength. To my four wonderful boys, you have brought such richness into my life. And to George, thank you for always keeping me grounded in the reality of our existence, as well as in the awe of it.

All: We would especially like to thank Sarah Stanton, senior acquisitions editor, for her keen insight regarding the significance and timely nature of this project. Sarah is an important ally. We would also like to thank Carli Hansen, assistant editor, for her logistical skills, her excellent handling of crucial details, and her speedy responses to all of our questions and inquiries. And last but not least, we would like to thank Alden Perkins, senior production editor, for her shepherding this important project to completion. Thanks to Sarah, Carli, and Alden for making this entire process move seamlessly.

INTRODUCTION

For the Love of Our Sons

George Yancy

A man was expected to behave like a man. I was expected to behave like a black man—or at least like a nigger. I shouted a greeting to the world and the world slashed away my joy. I was told to stay within bounds, to go back where I belonged.—Frantz Fanon

You were born where you were born and faced the future that you faced because you were black and *for no other reason*.—James Baldwin

To be a black man is to be marked for death.—William David Hart

While it is true that I'm not a *mother* of a Black son or Black sons, I know what it means to be a *Black son* of a loving mother, a loving *Black* mother, a mother who raised me and cared for me despite the objective, measurable odds that were against me from birth. There are millions of other loving mothers, across racially marked divides, of Black sons who are painfully aware of what it means to give birth to and raise Black sons in a world that marks their sons from birth as "unwanted," as "problems" who are already so-called criminals, uneducable thugs, and surplus bodies.

Like many Black boys and men, I have experienced these misperceptions about my identity and intentions firsthand. While I have shared this story in a *New York Times* op-ed,[1] it seems particularly apropos within a text that brings together collective maternal voices on behalf of Black sons. During the 1970s, I had an interest in astronomy. So, my mother decided to buy me a telescope. I spent hours searching the heavens. I would look at the moon and map its craters. I would also keep track of Jupiter's moons. On one special night, I turned my telescope on what appeared to be an orange colored object. It turned out to be Saturn. That was a beautiful sight. I was enchanted. Keep in mind that I was just a teenager and lived in a low-income area in North Philadelphia; in fact, I was a project kid, a kid who was supposed to settle for mediocrity. One night as I was coming down the hallway stairs with my telescope, a white police officer saw me through a small window leading to the outside. He peeked into the window. I opened the door and the first words that came out of his mouth were: "Man, I almost blew you away!" He thought that I had a weapon. The words made me tremble and pause. In retrospect, this was something more than an existential death shudder that is due to our finitude; this was an experience of potential (and in so many cases, actual) existential limitation punctuated by being Black within an anti-Black world. Had I been "blown away," my life would have been taken by someone whose job it is to serve and protect. My young and fragile body would have been shattered by bullets. It had already been shattered by his white gaze. After all, how could he "see" that this Black male teenager had a telescope? He was inculcated by racist assumptions to think otherwise. A Black boy with his telescope seemed to be beyond his imaginative range.

When it comes to Black male bodies, various benign objects carried can become "weapons." As in the case of twenty-three-year-old Amadou Diallo (1999), who was shot at forty-one times and hit with nineteen bullets after white police officers mistook his wallet for a gun, I would have been killed for possessing a "weapon" that was really a telescope. My guess is that the white police officer would have been found innocent because he had "reasonable" cause to think that I posed a threat. After all, or so the racist logic goes, who the hell would have thought that a Black boy would have a telescope (and not a gun) in the projects? Imagine the reaction, the pain and sorrow, the rapid heartbeat, the struggle to breathe, the hopelessness that my loving mother would have felt upon finding out that her Black son had been killed. Imagine the irreparable rupture in her heart, the irretrievable life force that permeated my embodiment, that agonizing need to say, "I love you!" once again before I was killed. Again, I'm not a *mother* of a Black son or Black sons, but I know what it means to be a *Black son* of a loving mother, as one of the beloved of my mother's life.

I will never know what it is like to be pregnant with a Black son, to give birth to a "problem," something that white society superimposes specifically upon the Black male body and the Black body, more generally. Mothers of Black sons, however, *don't* give birth to problems. That is a lie that functions to buttress the "sanctity" of whiteness, to instill in white people an insouciant disposition toward the dehumanization of Black bodies, Black sons. The conception of Black people as problematic and as inferior sub-persons is deeply embedded within the history of white America. For example, Khalil Gibran Muhammad notes that in 1836, William Drayton, a Southern white lawyer, argued in an anti-abolitionist pamphlet that "personal observation must convince every candid [white] man, that the negro is constitutionally indolent, voluptuous, and prone to vice, that his mind is heavy, dull, and unambitious."[2]

Frantz Fanon, who was painfully aware of how the Black *imago* or image functions within the white imaginary, wrote, "Sin is Negro as virtue is white. All those white men in a group, guns in their hands, cannot be wrong. I am guilty. I do not know of what, but I know that I am no good."[3] This is precisely what is communicated still to Black male bodies as they are stopped-and-frisked by white state authority that has the power and permission to keep Black male bodies within bounds. NYPD's stop-and-frisk is a twenty-first-century mode of de facto segregation, a reenactment of a manifestation of Black Codes that were installed in the American South to keep Black male bodies under surveillance. As Fanon suggests, because of the bombardment of so many images, messages, and lies, the internalization of a problematic racist gestalt can result: *"I am no good; I must have done something wrong."* With piercing irony, Patricia Williams writes, "How precisely does the issue of color remain so powerfully determinative of everything from life circumstances to manner of death, in a world that is, by and large, officially 'color-blind'?"[4] She continues, "What metaphors mask the hierarchies that make racial domination frequently seem so 'natural,' so invisible, indeed so attractive? How does racism continue to evolve, post-slavery and post-equality legislation, across such geographic, temporal, and political distance?"[5] Similarly, the convict leasing of

Black male bodies after the Civil War and its profit-making motive is reminiscent of the contemporary proliferation of private prisons and the profit made from them. Within both contexts, the Black male body is marked, imprisoned, and commodified.

As stated above, mothers of Black sons *don't* give birth to problems. They give birth to children for whom they would give their very lives; they are the first to feel the movement of, in this case, Black life literally in their bodies, a kick, an arm, a movement that signals vibrant existence. That movement from the inside is something that we, as men, will never know. It is an intimacy that places the mother in a special epistemic, physical, and emotional relationship to her child, her Black son. It is our *being-in* their bodies that constitutes the matrix (in Latin, "womb") within which we first come to experience safety, to hear the beautiful rhythm of a heartbeat that is not our own, a voice that resonates through our bodies. I imagine that the process of being pregnant speaks to one of the most profound and mutually rich forms of relationality. It is this primary and intimate relationship between mothers and their *Black sons* (and, of course, Black children and children of color, more generally) that bespeaks a different urgency of loving concern, a different existential gravitas that is infused with powerful feelings of desperation, frightfulness, protectiveness, toughness, and yet unspeakable joy.

We are all born finite; none of us will remain here forever. That is part of the human condition, part of an existential contract, as it were, that we sign upon our arrival. We are all bound for the grave. This deep existential feeling is what Cornel West calls the "death shudder." He writes, "I experienced it as a deep anxiety or dread connected to the overwhelming fragility of life in the face of death."[6] He asks, "How do we live with the idea that we are always tantalizingly close to death?"[7] I have personally experienced what West characterizes as the death shudder. There are times when my own finitude grips me, leaving me deeply perplexed and literally shuddering. So, apart from the faith and hope that we might possess, apart from the metaphysical narratives that we use to make sense of our lives, of our mysterious presence here and now, we must face the transitory nature of our embodiment. However, that sense of vulnerability, that sense of finitude, that precarious sense of being here today, gone tomorrow is greatly impacted and magnified by how we are *raced*, how we are *racially* marked. Race adds a different dimension to the death shudder. Hence, a Black son faces death differently from, let's say, a white son, one who gains from unmarked privilege and the bestowal of "innocence." White sons are protected by a society that doesn't need to declare publically: "White Lives Matter!" There is no need to prove that the value of one's existence ought to be unassailable. His white life always already matters. His mother need not worry that when he shouts a greeting to the world that the world will slash away his joy. His white life will not carry the burden of being sullied by a "darkness" that will work against him despite his efforts to achieve, to succeed, to move through space effortlessly, and *to be*. His white life will not be *marked* for death. Like all of us, because he is finite, he will not escape the touch of death, the ineluctability of death. However, it is at the level of social exclusion, the level of historical brutality, the level of conscious and unconscious hatred, that Black sons have a different relationship to death. Unlike white sons, the death of Black sons is always already imminent because of a racist societal logic that says that they don't matter, that they are excessive, disposable. Black sons undergo processes of negative stereotyping that distort the integrity of their humanity, where they are stopped *because* they are Black, because they are believed "deviant" and "up to no good," where death seems to be the only answer to a life that is deemed inconsequential to begin with. As "social deviants," Black boys, teenagers, and men, that is, Black sons, carry the mark of being a white person's worst nightmare. Williams writes that "their social lot is made far grimmer by their having been used as the emblem for all that is dangerous in the world from crime to disease. The conceptual cloak that makes any white criminal anomalous in relation to the mass of decent white citizens is precisely reversed for black men: any black criminal becomes all black men, and fear of all black men becomes the rallying point for controlling all black people."[8] So, our Black sons are like a social cancer that metastasizes and negatively impacts the entire Black body politic, revealing the "diseased" state of Black America. On this score, white America is seen as "justifiably" protecting itself from possible contamination. The objective is to remain white, that is, pure.

When there is a weapon, as in the case of seventeen-year-old Laquan McDonald, in Chicago, Illinois, in 2014, the Black male body poses an additional threat; that is, the intensity of the threat to white safety is increased. That is, the "cancer" must be contained no matter the cost to Black life. For example, McDonald only possessed a small three-inch blade. And despite the fact that he walked away from the white police officers, one white police officer shot him sixteen times. Even as McDonald was already on the ground, he was being hit by bullets. The white police officer didn't see someone's child; rather, he saw a hyper-violent monster out of control and needing to be stopped, dead. Yet, who is the monster here? What is it that leads a white police officer to shoot a seventeen-year-old Black teenager sixteen times as he turns away? My assumption is that it has to do with the *specter* that the history of white America has created; the projected Black monster, the "nigger," that white America has convinced itself it can't live with and paradoxically can't live without. It is that paradox that constitutes the pathology of white America and, in this case, leaves mothers of Black sons in unspeakable pain and suffering.

These tragic deaths of Black boys and men have a terrifying regularity. In 1955, in Money, Mississippi, fourteen-year-old Emmett Till's body was mutilated; his face was disfigured into an unimaginable grotesquery. He was beaten, shot, and thrown in the Tallahatchie River. Think about the pain and horror that his mother, Mamie Till-Mobley, felt as she had to identify her Black son's body. In 2014, in Cleveland, Ohio, twelve-year-old Tamir Rice, another man-child, was shot and killed while in possession of a toy gun. How does a mother make sense of such a death? How does she process that her son was shot and later died after it took less than two seconds for a white police officer to determine that he was a "threat," not an innocent twelve-year-old boy playing with his toy gun? Why didn't the white police officers see him as a twelve-year-old? Imagine the pain of his mother, Samaria Rice, processing the reality that her boy was gone. Also, in 2014, in Staten Island, New York, white police officers surrounded forty-three-year-old Eric Garner as one white officer applied what was called a "choke hold," according to the city medical examiner. I can't imagine the pain of what it must be like for Gwen Carr, his mother, to listen to his cries: "I can't breathe!" Garner cried out those words of entreaty eleven times. Yet no one responded to his call for help. What is it about Black sons that render their voices, their cries unhearable? In 2015, fifty-year-old Walter Scott, in North Charleston, South Carolina, was shot in the back by a white police officer who lied about the facts of his being threatened by Scott and thereby needing to defend himself. Judy Scott, his mother, has to live the rest of her life knowing that her son was shot and killed like a wild animal that had to be put down—shot in the back while fleeing. Also, in 2015, forty-three-year-old Samuel DuBose, in Cincinnati, Ohio, was shot in the head and killed by a white University of Cincinnati police officer as he attempted to drive away from the police officer, not as he attempted to run over the police officer, as was said. Video evidence does not show that the officer was in danger of being run over or being dragged. Audrey DuBose, his mother, will have to think about that shooting for the rest of her life. Perhaps she looks at pictures of her Black son's young smiling face, the fragility of a young body being held in her arms. In 2012, seventeen-year-old Jordan Davis, in Jackson, Florida, was shot and killed by white male Michael D. Dunn after he asked Davis and his three friends to turn down their music. The policing of Black bodies is not new in white America. In this case, it was a case of aesthetic or sonic policing. Why didn't Dunn just leave them alone? After all, all of them were in a parking lot of a convenience store, a public place where one moves in and out quickly. Perhaps, had Dunn said nothing, he would not have "seen" a gun, a gun for which no evidence has been uncovered. Lucia McBath, Jordan's mother, will have to live with the reality that her Black son was killed because a white man feared for his life, based upon what the evidence points to— a mere fiction. Also, in 2012, seventeen-year-old Trayvon Martin,[9] in Sanford, Florida, was pursued and killed by George Zimmerman. Martin, Zimmerman believed, was "suspicious" and "up to no good," though he possessed only a bag of Skittles and a bottle of iced tea. It was sufficient that Martin was a Black male for him to be in the "wrong place." Then again, is there any place in white America where the Black male body is not in the wrong place? After a struggle, Martin was shot and killed by Zimmerman. Like Davis, Martin might still be alive had Zimmerman left him alone. Had he done so, Martin would have headed back to his younger brother for whom he had gone to the store. Out of the above tragic situations of Black sons being killed, and so many others not considered here, I recall most vividly the uncontrollable tears of Sybrina Fulton, Martin's mother, which we all witnessed on the news. I thought of the knot in my stomach that could not be untied. I wept as I listened to what may have been Martin's last cry for help. The tears flowed as I thought of Trayvon, his mother, my Black sons, and other Black sons who are marked for death in an anti-Black America.

As stated, the above tragic deaths transcend the existential death shudder and locate the Black male body within the space of a limit that is fundamentally linked to white power and white paranoia; it is not a vulnerability suffered because all things are finite. Rather, it is the Black male body that is multiply vulnerable because its *raced* identity is deemed "dangerous," and its life is deemed "disposable."

I was recently talking with my nine-year-old son, and he mentioned to me that he and the other children on his bus had witnessed a man being arrested. Traffic had stopped as they watched him being brought from his home in handcuffs. In my head, I was debating whether to ask, "Was he Black?" And then I thought that my son might respond, "Why did you ask that?" I didn't want to disclose inadvertently the assumption that I was already struggling against. The assumption was in my head, partly because it is Black men who are disproportionately shown in the media being arrested. I knew the origin of the assumption. So, instead, I said, "Describe the man." My son said that he was African American and had dreadlocks. He also added that each time the bus passes that street that he and his friends think about what they saw. What impact will this have on my son, especially as he doesn't see actual arrests? And as there are also white kids on his bus, I wonder how they will be impacted. How will that scene impact all of the young boys and girls, white and Black, who witnessed that Black man being arrested, the one with dreadlocks? They may come to forget that scene. Yet, unconsciously, it will linger, perhaps even be "confirmed" by narratives that mass media will continue to bombard them with when it comes to Black males. Our young Black sons are impressionable; they process images; and, the hidden meanings that are communicated may someday haunt them. As another one of my (at the time) elementary school sons once observed, "Why are all the boys who are taken to the office *dark* boys?" Already, connections are being made, lives are being impacted, and there are glimpses of an anti-Black future being foreshadowed.

Returning to pregnancy as one of the most profound and mutually rich forms of relationality, I argue that the knowledge that mothers possess when they learn that they will give birth to Black sons carries an additional weight. Given the "threat" to white America that Black sons pose, imagine what it means for a mother to rub her abdomen knowing that she will give birth to a Black boy, a Black son. Perhaps there is a profound moment of hoping that it is a girl, which is not to say that

Black girls/women are not burdened by suffering and pain, especially on multiple axes. Perhaps there is a deep shudder that this Black boy is only destined to reach age twelve like Tamir Rice. Perhaps there is fear that he will be cut down as he listens to his music or walks with Skittles, or perhaps blown away as he searches the heavens with his telescope or reaches for his wallet. The relationship between mother and son is already precarious; as her son grows up, his life can be snatched from her because he is Black and for no other reason. White mothers of white sons don't worry about the fact that their sons are white. The world welcomes them, confers upon them forms of immunity that Black sons are denied in the womb. Think of the tears of mothers of Black sons who know the score, even as their sons are in the womb. Think of the anticipated dread of losing that Black child before it is born. Here is a case where rubbing the abdomen can function as both a loving, welcoming gesture and yet an early gesture of saying goodbye. It is that sense of pain and sorrow and yet joy and hope that constitutes the genesis of this book.

The book that you hold in your hands is a book filled with pain and joy. During the initial phase of this project, after asking individuals to contribute, I hit a potential roadblock that I had not anticipated. Some of the mothers said to me very clearly that they *could not* participate because of the sheer weight of what writing about the topic entailed, the pain of recalling all of the recent killings of unarmed Black sons by white police officers and the pain of meditating on the possible encounter of their own loving sons with said police officers. In their initial refusals, I could hear the weight of what I was asking of them reflected back to me. How could I have missed this, how could I have failed to realize that I was asking for levels of exposure that may have been too much to bear? There was a part of me that understood how writing about *their Black sons* was deeply emotional and how they had undergone forms of vicarious trauma through hearing about so many deaths of Black sons. Yet, I knew that they had to voice *their pain*, the pain that all of us who love Black sons (our Black sons) were experiencing collectively. There was a need for release. So I asked those who felt that the task was too daunting to face that pain, to meditate on all of that suffering, and to confront it and put it into words. I assured them that mothers of Black sons around the world needed to hear what *they* had to say. It was those words that carried them through; it was that mutual understanding that they stand together and that their voices would function cathartically, a process of articulating the sorrow, touching the pain and the fear, and celebrating the love.

The authors within this book are all too aware of what it means to love Black boys, Black sons, and Black men. We have seen more and more mothers of Black sons in a state of crisis and profound grief as each lost her unarmed son to white police violence or to their proxies, and those who took it upon themselves to control all things Black, "dangerous," and that are "blights" on America's white "innocence." This book is one of hope, love, honesty, vulnerability, and fear. It is a book that captures the voices of mothers of Black sons that move across race, age, religion, and nationality. To utilize the full range of forms of giving voice to the emotional weight and uplifting joy of loving Black sons, the contributors use narrative reflections, essays, poems, and letters. In short, there is no single monolithic voice and no single writing style. However, as a collectivity, the voices speak to an untiring and unyielding love of Black sons. Despite the past history of that peculiar institution known as "American slavery," where sons and daughters were separated from their parents and from each other, where the bonds of love had to be limited, in so many cases, to the womb only, and despite the past onslaught of white terror experienced by Black bodies (mostly Black sons) under the bloodlust of white American-style lynching, the voices within this text capture something of an ongoing tragic narrative of early *separation*. What are the psychic scars that mothers of Black sons experience after their sons have been shot dead with white police impunity? What happens to the minds and hearts of mothers of Black sons when those mothers are uncertain if they will ever see their sons again on any normal day of saying "goodbye" or "see you later"? What occurs when a mother realizes that no matter how strong her love happens to be, it is not strong enough to protect her son from the perception of those who will see him as "dangerous," as "unlovable"? What happens when Black sons move through the world, living with a sword of Damocles hanging over their heads? As a mother, how do you release your Black son into a world where he is perceived as a threat, as too big for his age, as a man when he is just a child? So she kisses his face, feeling in her heart the power that her love and her hope will return him to her safely, no matter the odds against it. She knows of his possible physical death, but she also worries about his psychological death, that fear of knowing that her son could come to see himself as white society sees him—*as a problem*. No mother should have to worry about her son because he is raced as a "problem," as a "brute," as a "nigger." Yet, that is the reality of what it means to love Black sons in an anti-Black America. So the mothers within this text love hard; they love with honesty; they love with hope; they love with daring and audacity; and they love with fear and trembling. And yet, they love. The book that you hold is a book about love; love for Black sons. It is a book that is captivating by its descriptions of an outpouring of indefatigable affection, a form of expressed love that feels indestructible and boundless in the face of an American history that refuses to keep our Black sons safe.

I

Reflections

I

BLACK MOTHER/SONS

Sara Lomax-Reese

I will not allow this twoness to fracture my mind, body, and spirit. W. E. B. DuBois nailed it back in 1903 when he wrote: "It is a peculiar sensation, this double-consciousness, this sense of always looking at one's self through the eyes of others, of measuring one's soul by the tape of a world that looks on in amused contempt and pity. One ever feels his twoness, an American, a Negro; two souls, two thoughts, two unreconciled strivings; two warring ideals in one dark body, whose dogged strength alone keeps it from being torn asunder."[1]

One hundred and thirteen years later, DuBois's words ring with a truth and clarity that haunts me as the mother of three Black sons. I am utterly confounded when I confront this timeless struggle that Black mothers have wrestled with for hundreds of years: how do I empower and encourage my sons to walk tall and fearlessly in the world, but arm them with the reality that in America Black men are often considered criminals at first sight rather than students, sons, fathers, men—full human beings?

Any illusion that, with the election of our first Black president, America has evolved beyond its racist roots was shattered in a quiet neighborhood in Sanford, Florida, in 2012 when Trayvon Martin was stalked, shot, and killed by George Zimmerman. My knee-jerk reaction was to try and find something about this boy that separated his experience from my three sons, two of them close to his age. But at the end of the day, what was so completely terrifying was the reality that Trayvon Martin could have been any Black teen, including my son: the jaunt to the local convenience store for some junk food (check), the hoodie (check), the cell phone conversation chronicling his every move (check). He was a young kid doing what young kids do and ended up gunned down, dead.

Listening to my then fourteen-year-old son and his friends trying to make sense out of this one was absolutely heartbreaking. "Glad I don't live in Florida," said one. "I'm not wearing any more hoodies," said another. And when I asked my son Elijah what would he do in a situation similar to Trayvon's, he said he would confront the person stalking him. "No, no, no," I said, "that's what got Trayvon killed. The goal is for you to get home alive." But the twisted reality is that there is no credible plan to give your child in this kind of situation.

I recently had the opportunity to attend an interview between Tracy Martin, Trayvon's father, and Philadelphia journalist and WURD Radio talk show host, Solomon Jones. With a quiet, calm dignity, Martin shared the intimate details of his son's birth. He told of being the first person to hold baby Trayvon in his arms; the boundless love that engulfed him; the personal commitment to be his mentor, guide, protector, friend throughout his lifetime. He talked of their close relationship, even though he was separated from Trayvon's mother—weekends at the local basketball court, telephone conversations that always ended with "I love you." He was a committed, loving father, fully engaged in his son's life. Eventually, the inevitable came when he shared the heartbreaking story of the night Trayvon was murdered. Unlike me, sniffling with tears dripping down my face, Tracy Martin spoke plainly, with strength and determination, of the utter horror that shattered his family's life. I left that event in a fog of sadness and confusion. How could this man survive what surely would have killed me? Not only did he have to endure the absurdity of George Zimmerman's murderous fear, he had to confront a criminal justice system that did everything to justify his son's killing. The slander included: Trayvon had used drugs; he wasn't a great student; he had been suspended from school—anything to confine this young man to the box of "Black male criminality." And, therefore, the theory goes, he deserved what he got. In fact, George Zimmerman was just protecting his neighborhood from a "menacing thug."

But Trayvon was just the beginning. Over the past four years, the death toll kept rising: Jordan Davis, also in Florida; Eric Garner in Long

Island; Michael Brown in Ferguson; Tamir Rice in Cleveland. And the unfathomable reality is that even when caught on video or with eyewitnesses, in most of these cases, the killers, often police officers, were exonerated.

As the mother of Black sons, the harsh truth is that there is no sane answer for the insanity of racism. The weight of this brutal reality, while insisting that my sons can achieve anything, reach for their dreams, have boundless success, is at the heart of DuBois's twoness. It can really make you crazy—or depressed—or resilient.

Perhaps this twoness is at the heart of our creative genius. Throughout time, Black people have been innovative, creating brilliance out of chaos. From Negro Spirituals to Ragtime, Jazz to Hip Hop, we have figured out a way to transform pain into power. This is the message I try to marry with the inexplicable in an effort to empower my children.

I also want my children to believe in the innate kindness that exists in most people—another dimension of the twoness. Despite the realities of racism, discrimination, and injustice, I still have a deep and abiding belief in human decency. One day, my then ten-year-old son Julian asked me: "Is there any place in America where Black people are equal to White people?" Once again I was stumped. While I hemmed and hawed, trying to find an optimistic answer for my youngest child, I sadly concluded, no. This blunt answer, however, had some caveats. I asked him if he felt discriminated against in his day-to-day life. At that time he was a fourth grader at Germantown Friends, a Quaker school in Philadelphia. As he thought about it, he concluded that his friends and teachers treat him with respect and kindness. So my more nuanced answer was that people are generally kind and decent on a one-on-one basis. However, there are deep structural policies rooted in this country's historic avoidance of its racist past and present that have created institutional racism and inequality.

This was seen with profound clarity on March 4, 2015, when the Justice Department released its findings on the widespread corruption in the Ferguson, Missouri, police department and court system. It proved irrefutably that Black people were being over-policed, picked up on minor or manufactured charges that carried jail time and large fines, which were then used to fund the city. What better example of Michelle Alexander's theory that we're living in the "New Jim Crow"?[2]

Black people have always been an economic engine of the American economy. From chattel slavery, when America prospered on the backs of 250 years of free labor, to the Ferguson findings, our exploitation is a part of America's capitalist system. Our current reality is the natural extension of a nation built on DuBois's "twoness." Even as the phrase, "all men are created equal" was being penned in the Declaration of Independence, White men were conspiring to institutionalize the permanent dehumanization of Black men and women. That chasm between lofty democratic ideals and the daily practice of buying and selling human beings is the cancer that has metastasized into our current reality. Today, the promise of America still rings hollow for many Black Americans who disproportionately live in communities with the highest poverty rates, underfunded and low-performing public schools, and an often hostile police presence.

I think about my parents, who left West Philadelphia in 1968 to raise six children—three boys and three girls—in Bucks County, at that time, an almost all-White rural community about an hour north of Philadelphia. While I wasn't conscious of it then, my siblings and I were part of the "integration generation." When I look back and realize how there were just a few short years between the widespread, state-sanctioned terror of the pre-1960s and my arrival at an all-white elementary school in Perkasie, Pennsylvania in 1974, I am inspired by the general kindness that I received from teachers, students, and parents. Even still, while I don't have tales of cross burnings or beat downs, there was a palpable undercurrent of being "other." While seemingly accidental, the N-word made regular appearances. This was way before Black music, style, and culture was synonymous with cool. I am proud of the eight-year-old me that was able to navigate my personal twoness—a home that was defiantly Black, with conversations about race and racism discussed regularly, and a school life that was so deeply invested in whiteness that anything associated with the color Black was synonymous with wholesale inferiority.

My parents provided me with a powerful roadmap for raising children, especially Black boys, in a society firmly grounded in presumptive white privilege. While they undoubtedly feared for the well-being of their children, they gave us incredible freedom and independence to travel our own paths. As my mother used to say, "I'm going to surround you with the light." Essentially she was saying, "I can't control what happens to you once you go out into the world. It is in God's hands, the ancestors, and the power of the Divine." It was a way of surrendering to the unknown, a way to make peace with your worst fears. As I look at it now, as a parent, I think it was about mental survival.

Their weapon for arming us against the macro and micro aggressions we faced in our daily lives was Black art, culture, family, and history. Our home was filled with vibrant paintings, soulful music, and heated conversation that reflected the complexity, genius, and diversity of the Black community. My parents were intent upon exposing us to the brilliance of Blackness through classic stage plays like *Purlie*, *The Wiz*, and *Black Nativity*. They would pack all six of us into the car to go see Stevie Wonder or The Temptations or the Edward Hawkins Singers. Annual trips to Jamaica exposed us to life in a Black nation where Blackness was the norm, not the exception. Weekly jaunts to West Philly for Sunday dinner at our grandmother's house provided psychological, spiritual, and physical soul food. A deep exhale. These moments allowed us to shed armor we didn't even know we were carrying.

My hope is that my husband and I are sowing similar seeds of pride and possibility in our sons, creating a wellspring of consciousness embedded deep inside their minds, bodies, and spirits, ready to be tapped when needed. This is our attempt at unifying the negative aspects of our double consciousness—the twoness—that for centuries has sought to fracture the souls of Black folks.

2

ONCE WHITE IN AMERICA

Jane Lazarre

For Adam and Khary

> *Black body*
> *swingin in*
> *the summer*
> *breeze*
> *strange fruit hangin from the poplar trees*[1]

It was 1969 and 1973 both times in early fall when I first saw your small bodies, rose and tan, and fell in love for the second and third time with a *black body*, as it is named, for my first love was for your father; always a word lover, I loved his words, trustworthy, often not expansive, sometimes even sparse, but always reliable and clear. How I—a first generation Russian Jewish girl—loved clarity! Reliable words—true words, measured words, filled with fascinating new life stories, drawing me down and in. The second and third times I fell in love with *black bodies* I became a black body, not Black, but black in a way, I'd say, without shame and some humor for mine is dark tan called white. But I am the carrier, I am the body who carried them, released on a river of blood.

Am I black in a cop's hands when he is pushing, pressing hard for dope or gun, or a rope or a knife or a fist? I am not a *black* body, yet my body is somehow, somewhere, theirs—Trayvon's, Emmett's, thousands more at the end of a rope's tight murderous swing, *black* as a night stick splits my head, shatters my chest, *black* as a boy not yet a man walking toward a man with a gun, suddenly shot dead, a just-become man, walking down the stairs toward a gun, *black* as a tall man, a big man, looking strong but pleading for his breath, killed by choking arms and bodies piled on top of his head.

Walking the sidewalks of my city in the morning, I dodge white dads' bikes daily, their little toddlers strapped into a back seat, and I don't mind as riding in the street or wide traffic filled avenues does seem a dangerous way to get to nursery school. Later in the morning, when I am still walking, the white fathers or mothers bike by me again, now with the back seats empty. I look around for police, wondering if there will be a ticketing for riding on the sidewalk, since no child's safety is at stake. No cops in sight.

My great-nephew, young and Black and not fully grown, was stopped and handcuffed by police a month ago for riding his bike on the sidewalk, his often glazed eyes glazing more deeply now.

Once I wrote a story—a black man named Samuel, enslaved in Maryland's western shore, 1863—I drew him in words.[2] His death was terrible and vicious, his body dismembered by the man who called him property, the crime—impregnating the man's daughter—a woman I called Louisa. I named her in part for a strong friend I wanted to conjure by my side as I wrote, but she was based on a real life young woman who lived in actual history, a woman named Jane, the same name as my own. Samuel's death was so brutal I had trouble reading my own words out loud, or even to myself at times, though I had written them: a slow dismemberment, piece by precious human piece, this nearly unspeakable violence also taken from reality, a horrific reality I had read about in books about torture during slavery, an image that refused to leave my mind, especially in the dark or when I closed my eyes. I watched him die with Louisa, and with Ruth, Samuel's mother, a character based in part on my mother-in-law, granddaughter of an enslaved American, and my close friend for more than forty years now, and I tried not to hide my eyes from the brutal human dis/memberment—the belief that they could erase his memory, his life as a man, yet thinking in this way to preserve the memory of his *crime:* a black man, enslaved, fathering the child of a young white woman who loved him. I called the novel, *Inheritance.* I wanted to claim the terrible history of my country, to honor the necessity of collective memory. I want to assert the power and capacity, the necessity, for human empathy and the deeper than skin-deep identification that comes with love.

My words telling Samuel's story in 1861 are almost as close to myself as my body-carrying boys, my sons, whose keys, in 1985, or in 1991, finally in the door at night assuaged my panic, waiting, waiting, trying to contain the fears, not only of muggers but, yes, of police, fears I had learned about most specifically as I listened, as they did, to their father talking what is now known as *The Talk*: Never run on the street, not even on your own block to catch the bus. Always show your hands. Never fail to be respectful even if police are insulting and disrespecting you. They have sticks, and guns, and your job is to come home safe.

My son's best friend in college, proud of his new car, *stopped*—in front of our building in Manhattan, thrown up against a car—*and frisked*—years before this assault had become a legitimized method with a frightening name. Once white in America, I watched and listened as I had learned to do in more creative, soul-expanding ways—learning from my new family about African American history and culture—witnessing my older son, always a lover of music, his face filled with mixed emotions as he listened in a high school classroom to Louis Armstrong singing the searing lyrics and haunting melody of "Black and Blue"; my younger son loved poetry, and has almost the same name as one of the falsely convicted boys in the Central Park Jogger case, so he wrote poems about them—the animal names they were called, the possibility, later proven, of their innocence; searching for healing, I introduced him to African American poetry, a centuries long tradition of various and elegant forms, poems of lamentation, and of the grace of memory and of love.

Once white in America, I searched for space within myself to absorb new meanings—now, years later, meanings so deeply absorbed they are entwined inseparably with my sense of the world as it is, the self that I am. I watch the television film again, and again, of Trayvon's sweet face, of Michael Brown gunned down in Ferguson, Missouri, of Eric Garner, a man in my own city screaming—*I can't breathe*. I hear my husband's voice, after nearly fifty years of living in New York City his tones and even some pronunciations returning to the Southern sounds of his youth and childhood—*I remember Emmett Till. When he was killed. He was the same age as I was. I still remember it—how it felt to me then.*

I want to reverse the meanings of the song I heard sung last month, after hundreds of listenings to old records, then CDs, this time by Audra McDonald who sounded so like Billie whose songs she was singing, whose gardenia she played with, on and off, on and off her thick black hair, whose drink she drank, put down, sipped again, whose graceful walk she walked, but sometimes wobbled, nearly falling, whose pain and anger she spoke in shouts and whispers about nightclubs and shameful insults, haunting memories and white only bathrooms when you very badly need to pee, of desertions and abandonments of many kinds, Audra singing such perfect Billie you could swear you were in the club hearing Billie Holliday's tones, soft and low to contrast with the terrible words echoing through time, from mind to body to mind.

The bulging eyes, the twisted mouth . . .
Scent of magnolia sweet and fresh,
and the sudden smell of burning flesh.

Their new born silken flesh, the deep sea eyes, the graceful mouth— the first time I saw their faces, rose and tan, wide staring eyes, one, then a few years later the other—hearing their father's sigh of relief and cry of joy, the long, hard labors over, once, then twice, and me smiling and alive.

Skin darkened slowly as they grew into men. *Are you half black*, someone asked when one of them was a child. He looked down. *Which half?*

What color am I Daddy? I captured and preserved these words in another story: *I mean, you know, what color am I? Really? Am I black like you?*

Yes, Son, you are Black, like me.

Black men, body and mind, in this white, white country I write and rewrite.
It is 1863[3]
and 1968[4]
and 2008[5]
and still we wait
for the bodies
to stop
falling, for our minds
to slow like rivers
after a storm,
waters
darkened to rich
olive brown by moist soil
lifted,

surfacing, warm.

It was Mississippi, he was just my age and I was scared, and angry . . .

It is Staten Island, New York . . .

It is Ferguson, Missouri . . .

No one indicted, no one held to blame.

1 – 2 – 3 ---4 -- 5 – 6 – 7 – 8 – 9 – 10 – 11 – 12 – 13 – 14 –15—16—17—18--19

We chanted loud, *Women in Black*, United Nations Plaza, 1999, calling out slowly the times Amadou Diallo was shot for pulling out his wallet. His mother's voice in the vestibule where he was murdered, crying out his name—Amadou, Amadou—again, and again, and again.

Emmett Till's mother insisting on an open coffin. Mothers and fathers of Michael Brown, Eric Garner, Trayvon Martin, calling for justice but also for peace.

It is 2015 and I could list so many names. I would pray but I am *not a believer*, as people call us now, but I do believe, in action, in what has always been called struggle, in what I insist on calling faith, in the human capacity and responsibility to know and feel another human story. I witness my son, now a man of forty, marching from Washington Square Park, up 5th Avenue, across 34th Street, downtown on 6th, long renamed Avenue of the Americas, to One Police Plaza. He marches and shouts with colleagues and friends—*I can't breathe—Black lives matter.*

Weeks pass, only weeks, and more murders—Walter Scott, a fifty year old black man, captured on video, running fast from a white man who is wearing the uniform of a police officer but betraying the requirement to protect the innocent, who is shooting Walter Scott in the back as he tries to escape. And just when I think I have found some even partially adequate words to respond to the atrocities of 2015, Freddie Gray is killed in Baltimore. Indictments are brought against the six police officers involved, but like so many others I am left to wonder—will this essay ever be finished? Is it destined to incompleteness? How many new deaths will I, must I, find a way to include?

I believe in words. I am a mother/grandmother/writer/teacher/wife of a Black man for forty-six years/friend/Jewish American woman who loves color and still knows words can sometimes, might somehow be, could be a part of the way, to everything.

I am the tan woman whose sons are tawny amber autumn leaf and almond brown cedar umber spring earth brown, whose sons are Black men now, the woman whose young nephew walks dangerous streets and rides on dangerous sidewalks, whose young granddaughter is "mixed," but clearly not white, slowly discovering and naming her inheritance.

And right now, as I write in the early winter days of 2015, I want courage here, a collective call, a shared claim—I am the mothers and fathers of Black sons shot down on Northern streets and stairwells and highways. Whiteness *is* a social and political category created to embed in the mind a false description of the body, its purpose to confirm privilege and superiority, to deny solidarity. It is not me. I reject it. It is not you.

We can't breathe.

3

A BOTTLE OF MIKE BROWN AND ROBIN WILLIAMS

Shelly Bell

Protecting a black son requires a mother to wear many layers of armor. American ideals reinforced by the media perpetuate the notion that a black boy can be sick, but not sad. He can be angry, but not suicidal. Everything about being a mother raising a black boy tends to feel external. The emotional state of my son (outside of anger) doesn't get evaluated properly for purposes of safety unless I fight that fight. In the fall of 2013, anxiety flooded the room of the for-profit social service organization for which I worked. The CEO decided to visit our site to discuss restructuring. He stood chest-puffed and proud to meet us in person. For the rest of us, however, it was just intensely awkward. I remember tapping out of the conversation to the point of imagining everyone as mimes. I was completely unbothered by the phone ringing during the meeting until one mime/co-worker roped in my attention from across the room with a weird eyebrow furl and a "can I talk to you for a minute" head jerk. I tipped out of the room with a Baptist church "excuse me" kind of motion of the index finger raised slightly above my head. I am not particularly religious, but my body reverts to ancestral muscle memory from time to time. "Someone from your son's school is calling," she explained. As I approached the phone, my anxiety shifted from concerns regarding the future of my employment to wondering if being black has affected my son today.

Josiah (age ten at the time) had been labeled as one of the "good black boys." He's smart, quirky, lovable, always smiling, and appears non-threatening. I tried to convince myself that the call was just another case of "Ma, I fell on the playground" or "Ma, I don't feel good." Josiah's quirky black boy pass makes me no less worried that his tokenized aura will fade when we least expect it. In moments like these, optimism is my go-to weapon. "Hi Ms. Bell, this is the school counselor. I am calling you because Josiah stated that he was having suicidal thoughts and he has a plan for how he would do it. When students state that they have a plan for suicide we cannot release them to go home. We need you to pick him up." My chest sunk. My breath ran out of the room. A wave of emotion blanketed me like being tucked into a bed I didn't even know I was sleeping in. Josiah had been suffering from episodes of depression since his grandfather's death in 2010, but suicide was never a topic of conversation. He usually worked with a consistent counselor at the school, but this was a different counselor calling. Both of the counselors for a school of majority minority children were white women. Holding the phone in one hand and my eyes with the other, the tears started to flow; oxygen returned to my brain and all I could say was "what?" The counselor went on to explain that he had gotten upset during class and began scraping his arm with a pencil and crying. One of the students saw this and told the teacher, then the teacher sent him to the counselor. In the wake of the CEO being in town to talk about restructuring (aka how to make more money), I feared that the mother of a depressed/oppressed black boy is less of his concern. Disclosing that my son has expressed suicidal thoughts at school felt uncomfortable, but the fear of losing my job because the white male CEO may or may not feel that simply saying "my son is sick" is a "good enough" reason to leave pushed me to make the decision to do so. After having conversations on various class levels with people of color noting that certain aspects of mental health struggles (including addressing mental health with therapy) is "white people stuff," I also feared disclosing this to a few co-workers. Seconds split into halves. I swallowed my fears, disclosed the situation, and headed to my son's school.

When I arrived, Josiah was sitting at a long brown table in a private room in the main office. I immediately asked him, "Are you OK? What's going on?" "Yeah, I'm fine," he says. The counselor walks in and begins talking. She explained that prior to my arrival she had asked him if he was having any suicidal thoughts to which he said yes. Then she asked him "have you thought about how you would do it? And if so tell me how." Josiah shrugged and replied, "I would probably drink bleach." My first thought was, "Huh? Who drinks bleach to die?" And then I thought, oh my God, how many times has he thought of this? How many times has he walked by the bleach and considered drinking it? Should I hide all of the bleach in the house? He's been in the house alone with the bleach. Was he thinking of drinking it every day? I sat with him to comfort him. Black boys need their mothers to be standing soft towers of love. Both security blanket and light house. I had to evaluate that this situation is indeed about his mental health as a person and not only as a black boy, and then find a solution that would address him as a person who is undergoing a set of powerful experiences, human emotions—not a black boy with aggression issues.

The counselor informed us that if a child identifies a plan to commit suicide, then they have to undergo a psych evaluation before they can return to school. The counselor attempted to help us find an appropriate place to take him for the evaluation. After making a few calls and walking in and out of the room asking me various questions about insurance, the counselor proposed a few places she had in mind. Most of them were overnight facilities. She advocated strongly for one place, but they didn't have any open beds. She insisted that I keep calling them back to check. Then she mentioned an organization in Washington, DC. None of the things I had heard about this place were good. When I asked a question about the facility, she made mention that this place would be a great fit for Josiah because it's "urban." I looked at my son, then looked at her and thought which part of this quirky kid does she deem to be "urban"? "Unless you define urban as black, there's nothing urban about Josiah," I replied. We lived right down the street from the school. The Fairfax County side of Alexandria, Virginia, would be a mix of urban and suburban, considering that we live in the Washington, DC, metropolitan area. However, our particular area, which is known as Mount Vernon (a few miles from George Washington's house), is not what I would consider "urban." The fact that she needed to say that the facility would be a great fit for Josiah because it's urban led me to believe that she suggested it not because of where we lived, but because we were black. She quickly jumped to defense by explaining that she didn't mean it "that way." Maybe she felt like he could benefit from being in a facility where there are other black people or counselors that could understand black mental health. If so, she failed to express it that way, and it was clear that she probably could not understand a black boy with depression. Much like the co-worker's eyebrow furl that roped me back to reality, my facial muscles were doing a dance of emergency. The counselor's cards were beginning to show. Reality began to set in. Why did he need to go to an overnight facility? What she saw is a *black boy* with depression who needs a facility that can "handle" him. I thanked her for the information and then began to google and decided to take him to Children's Hospital's emergency services for the evaluation.

After leaving the school, I asked my son what was going on. He said that he was feeling very sad about something that happened in class, so he was drawing on his arm and crying a little, but he wasn't scraping his skin or trying to hurt himself. One of the kids saw him and the teacher sent him to the counselor. The counselor asked him if he felt like he was going to hurt himself or others and he said no. She then asked if he had thought about committing suicide and he said yes. And then she asked if he was going to commit suicide how would he do it. He nonchalantly said, "I don't know, I guess I would drink bleach." At this point, I am starting to see the cracks in the counselor's lens. She is required to ask him if he felt like hurting himself or others. If he answered no, then the next question should not be about his "plan" for suicide. She made it seem as if he came into the office saying, "I feel like killing myself and I would drink bleach to do it" as opposed to answering the questions she actually asked him. When she asked him if he had thought about committing suicide, it was not about *that* moment. He took the question to mean if he had ever thought about committing suicide in general, ever in his life.

I was devastated. How do I teach my son that almost every question asked of him is loaded simply because he is black? The child psychologist at Children's Hospital was shocked that the school required an evaluation for him. She enjoyed his jovial spirit and quirky jokes. She informed us that Josiah is dealing with depression (which we knew), but he is not a threat to himself or others. The idea of having to go to a hospital for a psych evaluation was traumatic in and of itself. I had to calm his fears about something being wrong enough that he needed to be hospitalized. When he returned to school I had a conversation with the principal and counselor. I requested that Josiah not work with this counselor again. We survived that school year just fine.

On August 9, 2014, Mike Brown was killed in Ferguson, Missouri. His body lay in the street for hours. My son, daughter, and I watched footage of everything happening in Ferguson. We did so day by day. I asked my son what he would have done. His answer was, "Well Ma, I probably wouldn't be walking in the street and if the police asked me to move I probably would have just moved." I didn't know whether to congratulate him on seeing compliance as a precaution or to give him a history lesson on how compliance does not protect black boys. We had further conversations about what it means to be black and a boy in America. He couldn't quite grasp it because of his quirky kid pass, which provided him with a "you're not like the other black boys" safe space. This provision was something that operated without his conscious thought. I am often confused about whether I should feel accomplished by my combination of intellect and art that encourages the liberated quirky black boy character, or to beat myself up for possibly making him feel "too safe" in America.

On August 11, 2014, Robin Williams committed suicide. The person who made parts of my childhood happy became convinced that he was not happy enough to live anymore. He made a living by being quirky, awkward, emotional, and comical then ended that same life. Josiah and I didn't have much conversation about it. I asked if he had heard, he said yes, and that was it. People began expressing their sadness and sending condolences to the family via social media posts. Then there was a roar of division from the black community in particular. People wanted to keep the focus on Ferguson. Each day I saw more and more posts calling for people not to let the attention around Robin Williams's death deter the necessity to remain focused on Ferguson. The hashtag #BlackLivesMatter was tacked on to the end of posts calling to end the attention on Robin Williams's death and to refocus on Mike Brown's death.

I sat in front of my computer motionless, torn even. I even saw posts questioning whether or not Robin Williams's death was some type of ploy. Being black in America breeds a consistent level of distrust for media, so I understood why people would think such things. However, the division left me in internal turmoil. My son is depressed and a black boy. At any moment he could choke on the American Pie or be buried by his mental state. How can I protect him? My arms aren't wide enough. My legs aren't strong enough. My skin isn't privileged enough.

My locks aren't long enough to Rapunzel from the lighthouse to lift him to safety. Reminding my son of what it means to be a black young man while encouraging him to see his ability to be emotionally vulnerable and powerful is a fight that I haven't had much conversation with anyone about. It is a fear that settles in the pit of my stomach when he gets home from school every day. I never know how his experiences with typical teenage things will affect him emotionally. Recently, we have been using walks around the neighborhood as a coping mechanism for depression. The fresh air, green scenery, and physical movement provide a calming energy that returns his emotions to a state of balance. However, with every minute he is out of the house I am ping-ponging with the fear that his quirky character will not overshadow his blackness. That the police won't take time to notice his intelligence or manners. That my son won't recognize the world as his nemesis enough to know how to balance fight and future. Josiah is a bottle of Robin Williams and Mike Brown floating in an ocean of American realities. I pray I am lighthouse enough to guide him.

4

DARK RADIANCE

Becky Thompson and LaMar Delandro

If I forget to stop rushing cars,
let me know
If I forget to tame the lightning,
let me know
—Afaa Michael Weaver[1]

In the foundational book, *How Capitalism Underdeveloped Black America*, the late Manning Marable writes about the history of lynching, explaining: "Terror is not the product of violence alone, but is created only by the random, senseless and even bestial use of coercion against an entire population."[2] Marable's words help us understand that when one Black son is a victim of police brutality, all Black mothers, fathers, sisters, and brothers are affected. One killing in Missouri polices Black people in Texas, in Paris, all over the world. The murder of Emmett Till brutalized Mamie Till and all other mothers of Black sons. This is what terror means.

When the Ferguson decision solidified another period of terror, my friend Veronica Watson wrote me right away—her scholar-mother words spilling onto the page, red with anger and anguish. While both of us were stressed with other work, neither of us could go on with our days, words between us somehow a salvo. When I heard about *Our Black Sons Matter* my heart said yes . . . the call becomes a refusal to allow grief to swallow us whole. Late at night, I called my now adult son, LaMar, and asked him if we could write something together. Below are my words in regular script and his in italics.

When my daughter Crystal came down the stairs late last fall, saying, "you got it rough . . ." I knew what she was referring to without her having to finish her sentence—the dangers facing my non–gender conforming, hoodie-wearing African American/Southern Ute activist daughter in Boston and my six-foot-three dark-skinned gorgeous son who lives in Oakland. Neither safe, day or night. Reporting on the protest in Oakland following the Ferguson decision, LaMar tells me on the phone . . . "yeah, I drove by the community center where I know the demonstration would begin but knew I couldn't stay. Not safe for me, in case someone got violent." Just being there might put him in jeopardy. Not even safe to breathe.

In the *New York Times* I read of a police chaplain who describes mothers of slain sons as having "homicide eyes."[3] On the night after the Ferguson decision, Crystal and I went to the Black Lives Matter demonstration that began in Dudley Square (in a historically Black community in Boston). I scanned the crowd silently wondering who had lost a child or friend, who was worried about losing someone. Everyone looked worried. When it was too dark to see eyes, the feelings overshadowed us, sad, beyond sad, and angry. The organizers asked the Black elders in the crowd to come forward. I was relieved to hear from them first, the ones who have been able to make it through the decades. Many spoke. It was powerful, over 3,000 people. We all held up candles. We walked two miles to the Suffolk County Jail, as the organizers explained, "to be with our community there." The men in their cells stood at their windows—putting their hands up in silhouette, flashing the lights on and off. Our communication limited to hand gestures and lights.

When my son first came to me (when he was eight) the safety issues I most worried about were how to help him heal physically and emotionally from the welts on the top of his head from his white stepfather's belt; and from witnessing his mother being violated, moving way too many times, the disorientation of homeless shelters. At that point, he came up to my belly button, would burrow into my stomach in post office lines, under my coat in the winter. He wore hoodies in the summers and winter, still small enough (at least in my imagination) to be safe.

But when puberty began and his height shot up, I remember certain people crossing the street when we were walking toward them, my whiteness obviously not enough to protect them from their own paranoia. LaMar and I started to talk about which streets he could take, and not, when he went to get ice cream at night. I watched as some colleagues (who used to get way too familiar with LaMar's hair and head), started not moving toward him at all. I contemplated whether to turn an audio tape of Ernest Gaine's *A Lesson Before Dying* on or off when I would pick LaMar up from school—that razor-thin decision about what to tell Black children and not. How to arm and disarm them at the same time. My mentor, Dr. Reverend Katie Cannon, has said that raising Black children in this country means living with devastating contradictions—raising them for peace, teaching them about violence, asking them to open their hearts, teaching them to close down amidst daily physical and psychic affronts.

When he was thirteen years old, and at the beckoning of his biological mother, LaMar left our home and the multiracial community that was raising him, to live with his mother again in California. I fell into a deep place psychically, much of it not pretty. All hell broke out in his life—homelessness for extended periods; taking care of his little brother and sister when he should have been in school; being sexually molested by his white stepfather; hiding his writing and math skills in the high school he attended, fearing that being smart would not be seen as cool; losing all of the books and photographs and clothes I had sent with him; our losing contact for extended periods of time. In those years, I don't know how he found a way to not be arrested, to not get into drugs, to not get caught up in a gang. Sometimes the only word I have for that is grace. When LaMar and I finally found our way back into each other's lives again, my words got to change from "I lost my son" to "we were torn from each other." Many tears between us. And healing, too.

What being LaMar's ("second," "adopted," "chosen"—no words really fit) mother has taught me is that police brutality is only one of many dangers he faces. This is one of the hardest things for me to wrap my mind around. For many Black children, there is no safety in the home or on the streets, and that danger in the home often drives them out. The prison system is a huge part of the problem, robbing children of their parents, practicing acts of family destruction first honed under slavery. Heteronormativity just adds to this nasty mix as I worry when my daughter wears her hoodie outside, as gay bashing is only worsened by the violence of racism.

Given the many forms of violence LaMar has had to deal with, I am not at all surprised that the career he is focusing on now is with surveillance in a casino where there are clear "bad guys" and "good guys," where there is real-life video evidence of when people are stealing from the house and real-life protocol for intervening when people get out of control. I am not surprised that he was in a loving relationship with his teen love for five years and, even though they are no longer "together" they still support each other. I am not surprised that, when I asked him to write this essay with me, he immediately said "yes." His perspective, eloquent and to the point; his will to stay alive and thrive, fierce.

I have always tried to challenge myself mentally to find ways to adapt. I try to remember times when I have become mentally stronger, in charge of my own life, someone who is respected. I remember my grandmother telling me when I was younger, that I asked my stepfather, Bill, after he had beaten me, if he would love me more if I was white. When I moved back with my biological mother when I was thirteen, I was much bigger physically than when I left at nine years old. Still Bill tried to beat me. I remember asking him to whoop me every day so that I would get so mentally tough that nothing would hurt me anymore. He walked away after that.

As I have grown older, I have learned ways of moving forward. Physical strength gets you through a day but mental strength gets you through your life. After I left Boston I attended Oakland high school where everyone needed to be tough and big. If you don't have your head on your shoulders there you can lose your life. I wanted to be respected. It's hard to admit now but I wanted people to be afraid of me. I didn't want people to take advantage of me. There was an instance where I was trying to earn money. I would go to the dollar store and buy an eight pack of cookies and a six-pack of soda. I would sell it, a cookie and a soda for a dollar, and people would buy it (since that was cheaper than what you could get at the school). Not too many people were selling legit things. But whenever there is success, negativity will counteract it. In PE you put things in your locker. I found someone robbing my locker. I caught him. He was a smaller person. I was physical with him. I hit him . . . he tried to hit me back. I wanted to show everyone I wouldn't let anyone take advantage of me. I put him in a chokehold and kept him in it. But then it hit me. What I was doing was against everything I had stood for in my life. That had been my worst fear. That was going to be my reality. But then I stopped myself. I let him go. I walked away. I wish I could remember his name. I wish I could apologize to him. I apologize to him every day. I apologize to myself.

In East Oakland, you gotta be tough, nobody can question you. You gotta have the best shoes, the most talent. I didn't have the best clothes, the best shoes. . . . I didn't have the finances for that. So I went the route of trying to be tougher. If I was going to be accepted in the school that is what I had to do. I had gone to so many schools before high school in Oakland—in Illinois, Florida, New York, and the Quaker school in Boston. I didn't sound like people from California. My education level was higher than the people in my grade. My teacher would be upset 'cause I would leave my finished assignments under the desk 'cause I didn't want to be seen as a nerd. I just wanted to blend in. I didn't want to be made fun of. These weren't my rules. I wanted to be smart. . . . but I couldn't be myself.

In Oakland there are places I don't go to even though I know people who live there. I can't afford to find myself in the wrong place at the wrong time. It is too real, every day. I don't know if I necessarily feel sad about these restrictions. You just find yourself trying to survive. You don't have time for that. I go home and go to sleep. That is the one place I can find some peace.

It is crazy the damage police do to Black youth, the damage we do to each other. I look at the cues for how things are set up. I think about how the media responded to the protests in Oakland after the Trayvon Martin murder and the Oscar Grant murder where he was shot at the Bart station. After he was killed, there was a demonstration. Hundreds of people were sitting in front of the Marriott Hotel. When it turned toward evening, the media spokespeople said there might be a "state of anarchy." The media was not highlighting the positive parts of the protest—that it had been peaceful all day. The media was looking for what might happen. As it got dark, people continued to march and chant peacefully. I don't know who or how it happened but something broke and then police began arresting people for just being there.

It is really hard to keep your eyes on your goals. I didn't have a car then. I needed to take Bart. After the protests, Bart would not stop in certain areas. It was intense. Sometimes busses wouldn't pick people up at certain stops. It felt close to impossible to try to navigate, and survive while living in such an unjust world. . . . Sometimes I feel powerless myself. Then I think about what we can do, as people. We breathe, we sleep, we eat, we need water to live. What can we do to be as one?

When I was the Americorp supervisor for the East Bay, I remember there was a shooting that was followed by a lock down. I arrived at the school and began asking people . . . is everything okay? . . . But people were acting like nothing really happened. The violence and lockdowns were so common. It was like a normal day. Like a snow day in Boston. A regular snow day. All so normal. Something you almost expect.

It is so hard to reflect on this. I am living it. It is not a movie. Am I scared when I get stopped? Yes . . . we only hear the outcome. Another black male dead. I try to work hard within myself and do well . . . but Trayvon Martin was doing well in school but still, another deceased person. I just try to look at my life. To try to beat the stereotypes. I am 26 now. Almost 27. By 25, most African American males are in jail. I just try to push forward. To push into areas beyond color. Into spaces where people show love. And then to show other Black guys that they can make it. That I got out of a family where there was so much abuse. I got out. Others can, too.

Now, working surveillance at a casino, I work with police departments a lot. I find myself forgetting that police are human beings. Where I lived when I was younger in Oakland, police did not treat us in human ways. They were robots making sure we were afraid of them. It makes it very hard to feel safe when the police officer increases fear. I am more afraid if officers come than if they stay away. As a Black youth walking around I know there is a certain fear, on either side of the fence. Now, driving my car (which is a Lexus), I have been stopped a lot. Everything is legit but the officer feels the need to check me, or make me understand he is there. I carry myself well. I try to look at things from the point of view that we are all people. The spoiled apples make it hard for the police who want to be honest in their profession. Now the police are trying to build community. But a lot of youth think, well my cousin was shot by one of you, I don't know which one. One of you was in my house and broke down the door and it hasn't been fixed. The police are supposed to help us but they use the classic line, "we have to match fire with fire." People just want to live. They want to be free. They want to take care of their families.

My son's words move me beyond tears, to a place of awe—his discipline, his willingness, his wide-open heart. Two years ago, after he unfairly lost his job at Americorp and then he and his long-term girlfriend broke up, we almost lost LaMar. No bullet, no jail, just too much loss, too much violence, too much betrayal to hold in his one precious body. If I were to lose him, after all he has been through, I am not sure I could take it. That is one of the many things we have in common, LaMar and me, our feelings too raw, our hearts too open to (sometimes) feel like we can make it. But then LaMar started talking deeply about the emotional support he needed, and he started to find traction again. He found a new job, reconciled with his girlfriend, found a therapist who really listened, and I got him the fanciest new cell phone we could find, so he could call me, no matter what.

Now, I go to as many Black Lives Matter demonstrations as I can. I march with my daughter, and many of my students, who seem to know to stay close to me, way beyond when they graduate. And I keep scanning the eyes of mothers, hoping they can see mine, that they can see that I see theirs. In many ways, my analysis of the police violence as more than just a few bad apples, as systematic and historically rooted in slavery, comes from my white privilege. LaMar can't afford to walk around thinking that police, as a group, have been trained to see him as a target. I marvel at LaMar's stamina. I grieve for this world. Recently, I dreamt of LaMar when he was a toddler, before I even officially knew him. He was sweet, rocking in my arms like they were a swing set, to some soulful music, enjoying the sunlight, wrapped safely in his own dark radiance.

5

WHY BEING THE LONE BLACK FRIEND OF WHITES WILL NOT PROTECT YOU

Noliwe Rooks

Growing up in the overwhelmingly wealthy, white, and picturesque college town of Princeton, New Jersey, my son, Jelani, was pretty much the one Black friend any of his many white friends had. He was always popular in part because he had a wicked sense of humor, laughed easily, excelled at sports, and had college professors for parents. This last meant parents felt comfortable both having him in their home, as well as letting their children come to ours. He always had Black friends growing up, but they were rarely if ever as "accepted" as was our Jelani.

We were grateful that Jelani's childhood offered him a seeming level of comfort, if not the possibility for unqualified acceptance into our overwhelmingly white and affluent community. We breathed a bit more easily knowing that there were ways that where we lived kept certain types of social disorder at arms length. However, neither his stepfather nor I ever thought that his seeming intimate acceptance into the homes and lives of his white friends would shield him from the reality of racial stereotype, invective, or trauma when the time came. We prepared him as best we could. As his voice deepened, and his baby face sharpened, we worked diligently to strengthen his character, protect his psyche, teach him the ultimate value of an honest relationship with himself.

We did this because we knew that poor, or working-class, or urban communities were not the only places where Black boys are terrorized and traumatized. We knew that guns were not the only way to murder a Black male soul. And so seemingly prepared, we waited.

As the moments first arrived, and then intensified, we were not surprised. We were, however, overwhelmed by, and not prepared for, the consistency with which white adults, school officials, parents, and coaches all worked in seeming unison to turn every nasty, negative act of racial aggression aimed at our son into an opportunity to explain how he was responsible for the behavior of his white friends and classmates. He, we were told, pulled, yanked, and wrung the racism from the hands, mouths, souls, and bodies of his white teammates, classmates, and acquaintances. If he would just stop it, we were told more than once, if he would just change who he was, how he reacted, what he reacted to, they said, everything and everyone would be peaceful.

We began to learn this lesson when Jelani was twelve. One of his schoolmates called him a nigger. It was at the end of a softball game and their team lost. The boys weren't really that upset, but they started pointing fingers at each other and assigning blame. In the verbal sparring that followed, Jelani said something that made the other boys laugh at the child who had started the verbal fisticuffs. In response, as the other boys turned their laughter on him, on this young man who was Jelani's friend, he said, "Well at least I'm not a nigger." Jelani asked for an apology, said that wasn't funny. The boy turned red, said no, pushed Jelani. Jelani pushed back and as the rest of the boys circled them, calling for a fight, an adult arrived to break up the crowd and told both the boys to come to school the next day with their parents.

Jelani's stepfather and I arrived at the school expecting an apology. Instead we were told that both boys owed each other apologies. Apparently, Jelani was also in the wrong. If he had not made fun of the racial-epithet-hurling child, none of this would have happened. Jelani, we were told, would have to better learn how to treat his friends. One of the boy's parents, I don't remember which one, said that the white child probably learned that word from Jelani in the first place because, the parents assured the school principal, no one in their house talked like that.

Of course, by the time the meeting was over, we were all clear that Jelani apologizing to someone who had both called him a nigger, and then pushed him first, was not something that would be taking place that day, or any day. Nonetheless, a version of this same scenario of inverted responsibility happened so often that as time passed we grew less and less surprised.

The second incident took place a few months later. Jelani was in a science lab, and the students were told to pair up in order to complete a series of experiments. Though he already had a partner, a different young man in the class demanded that he be picked. Jelani said they had already paired up and was in the process of saying, "maybe next time" when the scorned partner took a ballpoint pen and rammed it into Jelani's thigh. The pen pierced the skin. Drops of blood formed around the wound. The pen clung to my son's muscle, seemingly floating in midair. During the meeting following that attack, the school principal told us that Jelani would have to learn that, while in his "community," treating others poorly might be acceptable, at his school, he had to treat his classmates with respect. Jelani, we were told, had hurt this young man's feelings when he declined to pair up with him, and since the pen-wielding boy had a history of emotional problems, clearly no one should think to hold him responsible. We all had a responsibility to make this young man feel like a welcomed part of the community. Jelani had not done that. There would be no apology.

As a result, what I remember most about raising Jelani in Princeton is not so much the charming shops, graceful houses, marauding deer population, or the liberal city government. No, what I most remember is how often my son was racially harassed, disrespected, and aggressed by his white friends and their parents. I remember how rare it was for his friends or teachers to protect him. I remember how perfunctory were the apologies finally wrestled. I remember the insistence, aggressively uttered and believed, that the various perpetrators were "good children" from "good families." I remember how fully we as family came to understand the intellectually suspect and morally ambiguous lengths so many would go to protect their investment in white supremacy.

The last time I know about that a supposed friend called my son a nigger, Jelani was a senior in high school playing soccer for his club team. One of his teammates screamed "Stop that nigger!" from the sidelines, referring to the opposing team's star player. When my son took offense, the coach, who had known him since he was ten, told him he was overreacting, to "calm down." My son's "friend" who did the hollering said, "But I wasn't talking about you. I don't think of you that way." But how that teammate would characterize my son did not extend to the unknown Black player on the field. For Jelani, that was a distinction without a difference. He never played for that team again.

In my house, we know that having a Black friend is not the same thing as *not* having stereotypical views of Black people. We know that being the lone Black friend who is surrounded and accepted by whites is *not* the same thing as a safe embrace or loving acceptance. At some point, we are going to have to sober up about the limitations of friendship and proximity as the main way to address racism or dismantle white supremacy. There are many more white supremacists in the world than we may be comfortable admitting. Some use racial epithets. Some do things even more subtle, like pass over Black candidates for jobs or educational opportunities. Some murder in cold blood. In my house we know, we understand, that it is not only a policeman's bullet that can crush a Black soul.

6

THE BOX

Tracey Reed Armant

It occurred to me during Jayden's first week of kindergarten. I held his hand and we fell in line with his class. Before we enrolled in the neighborhood public school, we examined the statistics. We knew that African American children were not faring well in the district and about half of the African American boys who started kindergarten would not graduate from high school. We understood completely that school would be a job for us. But we were up for the challenge. That morning, though . . . the first week of school, as I looked at the kindergarten classes, I was awestruck. I saw children who were happy and excited, who already loved their teachers, who were more than a little squirrely as they waited in line to get into the building. These kindergarten children were physically dwarfed by their fifth-grade schoolmates and by their own book bags. I watched all of the children, boys and girls, white, African American, Asian, and Latina/o.

I fought back tears as I looked on, knowing that some wouldn't make it to graduation. I looked at the little African American boys whose behavior and demeanor were distinguishable from the other children only in that they seemed more excited than everyone else to be there—not one of them seemed reluctant about going to school. Not one lingered uncomfortably long with his parent, not one held tight to his parent's hand until just before he reached the door, not one cried.

I watched them and their classmates as they marched into the building and I wondered: What happens to them in there?

I know their collective prognosis. I know that if the African American male kindergartners—these little six-year-old boys—were representative of the district, half would not complete high school. I know the statistics and so do their teachers and the teaching assistants and the security guards and the administrators and the cafeteria workers and the bus drivers and the custodians and the other parents. I wonder what that knowledge does to the effort that all of these adults put into little African American boys.

What does it mean for them that all of the adults in their lives know already that some of them won't make it to graduation? How do they shoulder that burden?

Knowing their prognosis matters. For me, it made me want to give them all big hugs as they went in; to offer them a counter-narrative; to tell them that they have a small window of time at school to seal their fates; to tell them that their behavior and demonstrated abilities these first few weeks of kindergarten would follow them throughout their school careers in ways that are not the case for their white classmates. I wanted to let them know that in a few short years, most of the members of this school community—their teachers, friends—may fear them.

I wanted to shout: IT'S NOT YOU! You, little six-year-old boys are not the problem. YOU are the victims. The world has created this outrageous set of circumstances with which you will have to contend and overcome, if you are to survive. Contending with these circumstances will be hard and will take will and effort and divinity, and overcoming them is way too big for little boys.

I knew that my son would do well in school. His deck was stacked such that he will likely graduate from high school and move on to postsecondary schooling. He will probably grow into adulthood and have a good job and a nice family. As much as I know that his deck is stacked, I also know that the other adults that he encounters throughout the day do **not** know that about him. To most adults he encounters, he is as likely to be in the large, crowded "will drop out and amount to little" category as he is to be in the sparse "this one has a chance" category. I knew inside that in school he would have to distinguish himself from the very people he is most like in order to be treated as if he has a snowball's chance in hell of succeeding. And I knew that being treated as if he can and will succeed is part of the battle.

When my son was little, one of our favorite bedtime books was *The Big Box* by Toni Morrison. We would read about how spirited children were often put into a "big box," disallowed the freedom to be bold and wild. We read about how uncomfortable adults can be with children's enthusiasm. We talked about how, despite the adults' proclamations that spirited children "just can't handle their freedom," these children COULD handle their freedom; they deserved their freedom.

I was completely devoted to the idea that children deserve to be free. As Jayden and I read *The Big Box*, I was adamant that I would parent in a way that would allow him to flourish outside of any boxes, and I would challenge any adult who attempted to "box him in." I was adamant and naïve. As I maneuvered preschool and saw and heard how African American boys are problematized, and as I watched the six-year-old boys go into school, and I knew the fate that would meet them—I began to build the box. I was strict—"don't say that, don't go there, come sit with me." I monitored his behavior carefully. I filled his days with school and books and his evenings and weekends with lessons and church activities.

As it became more clear, the differences between how I was accepted (a compliant, pleasant, polite girl) and how my son would be accepted (a compliant, pleasant, polite boy—an African American boy), I equipped the box with creature comforts. As I listened to the challenges that my husband still faces as an African American man, I decorated the box. As I considered the fates of Trayvon Martin, Michael Brown, Eric Garner, Johnny Gammage . . . I reinforced the box. It is a lovely box, just like those described in the storybook. The box is strong and stable and has all the creature comforts, but it is a box that I have intentionally built to try to keep my son safe because I fear his freedom.

I fear his freedom, not because he can't handle it, but because the majority of the adults and children, the teachers and police officers, the store owners and bosses who he encounters can't handle his freedom.

I know it's futile. I know that in order to truly live, he has to escape the box that I have carefully, fearfully placed him in to keep him safe. And this is the very deep, real conflict with which I parent.

7

WHITE MAMA, BLACK SONS

Heather Johnson

JANUARY, 2004 "FULL BLACK?"

I've known since I can remember that I will adopt someday. I can't explain it, it is not articulable, I just know.

I'm a professor of sociology at a well-respected university; I've studied and taught race, class, and inequality for much of my life. My husband and I fostered a black child for six years while we were in graduate school during our twenties. I've read almost everything published on transracial adoption. We've moved to a diverse and vibrant part of the country and positioned ourselves well to raise kids. We're about as equipped and prepared for parenting black children as any white people can be.

Still, I'm shocked when—on the phone with adoption agencies, inquiring about starting the process—every single person I speak with asks me the same exact thing: *"Full Black?"* I'm kind of stunned into silence with the crudity of the phrase. But I repeatedly gulp, and in response, as evenly as possible, answer, "Yes."

They always go on: "Really? You're sure? You'd be willing to adopt a full black child? What about gender? Would you be willing to adopt a full black boy?" I try to make my answer sound as absolutely-without-any-doubt-or-hesitation-100-percent-sure as I truly, deeply, absolutely know that I definitely am: "Yes!"

SEPTEMBER, 2006 "ARE THEY YOURS?"

Kyle and Owen are two-year-old twin boys, rambunctious as you can imagine, and thriving beyond belief. We adopted them from Haiti at age eight months. They surely are the most adorable children on the entire planet, and it appears that not just their mama thinks so. I cannot get through an aisle of the grocery store with my two-too-cute-toddlers without at least one (but usually several) people stopping me to "ooooh!" and "aaaaah!" over them.

I'm trying to master the art of politely avoiding eye contact and moving quickly through public spaces in order to simply live life with some efficiency. But I cannot go anywhere with these two without drawing a lot of attention to us. The attention is almost entirely positive (they are so darn cute!). But there's always a little edgy curiosity in there, too. White mama, black sons. I'm asked repeatedly, *"Are they yours?"* "Yes."

NOVEMBER, 2014 "WAS HE BLACK?"

We are dealing with the Ferguson decision. Today, walking into a Starbucks, Owen saw the front page of the *New York Times*. "The guy who was killed," he's looking right at me with his huge brown eyes, *"was he black?"* And I have to say, "Yes."

If you could have seen the look on his gorgeous soft brown face, you would have felt just as sick to your stomach as I did in that moment. He knows. If you loved my boy—even a little bit—then the look in his deep dark eyes would have tortured your heart and soul just as much as it did mine. I swear it. You'd be inhuman not to feel the pain of it.

Ten-year-old twin boys. Here we are. They are all energy, all zest, all live-life-to-the-fullest. They do everything to the maximum degree with the volume cranked up all the way, all the time. They are AMAZING. They are also getting a handle on the world. And, just as we knew it would, sure enough, the world is getting a handle on them.

It is hard, this thing. We knew it was coming, but that doesn't help. It is like a storm that you know is rolling in. You first just hear the forecast (and maybe wonder if it is true), then you feel it brewing in the air (and know it is to be), then you see it with your very own eyes (the sky turns gray, the clouds take over, the wind starts whipping). You can get ready, you can prepare, if you are lucky (or privileged, as the case may be) then you can even take cover (we are privileged; we work hard to provide as much shelter as every single resource available to us will allow). You can hunker down and you can do everything right. But it doesn't stop the storm from coming. It just rolls right in. It is bigger than us. It is more powerful than us. We are just there, relatively defenseless to its forces, attempting to cope as best we can. Hoping we are still standing for it to leave us in its wake.

Right now, I'm just hoping and praying and wishing and trying-to-believe that we'll somehow be the lucky ones—the parents of black boys who are lucky enough to watch them grow up and still be standing in its wake someday. I'm scared to hope for too much, but maybe someday we'll be talking together about the challenges of raising their children, our grandchildren.

For now, for today, we are just trying to get through this. This period of time when we watch as our precious sons grow out of being cute little black boys (adorable toddlers in a double stroller) in the eyes of the world. They grow up to be black men. Trust me, it is *hard* to watch.

We've hit the turning point. I've watched it happen. I've witnessed it firsthand. Over the past several months my sweet little adorable babies went from being perceived as just that, to being perceived just as I've long dreaded.

It has started.

I've been in the store and watched from a short distance as they've been followed. (Yes, already.)

I've heard it over the intercom system: "Security Alert. Section C. Security Alert." (Yes, already.)

I've stood behind them as they've been stopped in line, being perfectly obedient, but being questioned. (Yes, already.)

I've watched as they've been wrongly accused. As the worst has been wrongly assumed. As the fault has been wrongly blamed.

The looks. The hesitation. The ever-so-slight facial expressions. The too-quick-to-judge.

It has only just begun.

It doesn't matter that they go to an elite private school.

It doesn't matter that they are straight-A students.

It doesn't matter that they have white parents.

It doesn't matter that they are well traveled, worldly, well dressed, polished, polite, poised. It doesn't matter that their vocabulary is incredibly well developed, that they have eaten in fine restaurants, have met famous authors, have seen world-class performances, know the names of the classic European composers and philosophers, know how to shake a hand and look someone in the eye and use their best manners when needed. It doesn't matter that they are cloaked with class privilege and all of the advantages that go with it.

It doesn't matter that they are gorgeous and charming and organically charismatic. It doesn't matter that they are gifted and talented and have off-the-chart IQs and that the world should be their oyster. It doesn't matter. Still, they are followed, suspected, questioned, accused, judged, and—yes, already—feared. They are black.

Maybe you think I'm crazy to say this. Maybe. Maybe you should try being the mother of ten-year-old black boys for a little while, and then see what you think.

I can't be written off as an "angry black woman," because I'm not black. I am angry. And I am a woman. But I'll tell you this: I'm white, I grew up around white people, I know white culture, and I am embedded in whiteness. And what I see, feel, witness, and experience—it is real. If there is anything I know, it is that I know this is real. You can't tell me it isn't true because I am an insider and I know it is true.

My sons, no matter how authentically fantastic they are, are still black. We have to tell them the truth: you'll be judged quicker, you'll be perceived more harshly, keep your hands out of your pockets, keep your hood down, no fast movements, never run, racism exists, and it isn't to be messed around with. We'll do everything we can for you, but even we can only do so much. We are limited in how much we can protect you. No matter how much we try, no matter how much we love you, no matter how precious you are to us, no matter.

My sons are growing up to be black men. And they need to be prepared for what they could (almost certainly, will) encounter. We'd be gravely, woefully, unforgivingly failing them if we weren't to prepare them for reality. At ten, they are in process. And it is heart wrenching.

No matter how perfectly they present themselves, no matter how spectacular they are, they will be disproportionately extremely less safe than if they were white. Kyle and Owen's stellar reputations and hard-earned achievements and family privilege will not necessarily get them as far as they choose or could go. Because the world might just choose for them and against them—in ways that would simply not occur if they were white. That is what it means to be entangled in structural, entrenched, historic, and systemic racism. No amount of privilege—or charm, or charisma, or pure raw talent—can protect them from the fact that they are black boys.

In this way, despite how extraordinary they are, despite their stunning life stories, despite all that they have going for them, they are no different—hood up, or hood down—than any other black boy.

JUNE 2015 "AGAIN?"

Kyle and Owen turned eleven last month, and it has been a tough year for race relations in the United States of America. And now, the Charleston shootings.

Sadly, for me, but mostly for them, we're getting quite accustomed to these conversations. I've become—again, sadly—strangely adept at discussing these things in age-appropriate ways with my children. And let's be honest: when I say "these things," what I'm talking about is the tragic loss of black lives and the horrific racism all too often at the root of current events.

We can't shield them from reality. And I want them to hear the truth from me first—before they overhear someone talking about it, catch a glimpse of a television somewhere, or see the front page of a newspaper or website.

I knew I had to tell them today; I had tried to sort out my own emotions enough yesterday to prepare myself for talking with my kids about it today. So I got up early to make them their favorite muffins. And then, over muffins and milk, in our warm sunlit kitchen, I had two separate conversations.

"I have to tell you something," I began, and then I told them. Nine black lives lost, a historic black church in Charleston, South Carolina, twenty-one-year-old white male killer, gun, police search, caught and in jail, families and communities and me mourning, racism, the battle is not over, so much progress has been made, still a long way to go, and we—each of us in our family—you and me—need to be part of the push for change-for-the-better, we need to use our lives for good. And you are so deeply and enormously loved and cherished and valued.

Kyle couldn't contain himself as his angst spilled over. This kid, more than anyone I know (for real), gets it. In a rooted, comprehensive, overwhelming way, with, as C. Wright Mills would say, a complex inter-section of history and biography —he gets it.

I had barely finished my first sentence, "Kyle, sweetie, I need to tell you something horrible, on Wednesday night nine people were killed . . ." when he first said it, "Again?" I nodded as I continued, and he repeated it over and over in the short three minutes it took for me to tell him. ". . . in an historic black church in Charleston, South Caroli-na. . . ." "Again?" I'd nod and keep going, and he'd say, "Again?" and I'd nod and keep going. My throat felt constricted, like a thick choking feeling, looking him in the eyes—noticing for the millionth time how deep dark brown my boy's eyes are, how gorgeously creamy his dark brown cheeks are—and having to tell him this sickly thing. He seems way too beautiful for this ugly truth. But I know with every part of me that I have to tell him, and I have to do it right. I finished, waiting for his response, and he said again, simply, "Again?" "Yes." And I just stood there with him in a long silence. He finally said, "And in Charleston again? Why does it have to happen in Charleston? I love Charleston."

We've been traveling to Charleston every summer for the past four summers. And we'll be there again in just a few days. It is our family's happy place. No place is unscathed.

Owen is much more cut and dried. There isn't a lot of complexity to it for him. There is no gray area, things are right and things are wrong, and he calls it like it is. His reaction: "That. Is the definition of racist."

We hugged. They ate muffins and drank milk. All was okay. Sort of. Again.

I dropped them off for the day at—what they call—"Heaven On Earth" (basketball camp). They are beaming, self-confident, healthy, gorgeous boys. They fill up any space they are in with their larger-than-life charismatic personalities. Their life stories, unusual family makeup, their unique vantage point on the world . . . that just makes them all the more interesting to everyone they encounter everywhere. It is a lot.

They run off and are high-fiving and fist-bumping with their friends, the camp counselors, and the director. I lose sight of them in the crowd. I feel like I'm going to cry.

I'm scared for them. I'm scared for me. I thought I was equipped for this. I thought we were as prepared as possible to be white parents of black kids. In so many ways we were. But nothing could have prepared me for this.

It feels like a constant bombardment of traumatization. It feels like sharks are in the water, but I've 'gotta throw my babies—my most precious imaginable—into the deep end. They can swim better than any kid their age (truly: years of swimming lessons), they are strong (truly: in every way), they've got each other (truly: they've always got each other's back, they are never alone), but nothing—nothing—nothing—can protect them from the fact that they are black.

I knew it would be hard to be *white me* raising *black them*. I knew there would be a whole host of challenges to it. What I didn't know was the constant re-traumatization—*as a mother*—of standing defenseless, sending my sons out into the world, knowing that they have a disproportionally high chance, on any given day, of getting shot and killed, just because of the color of their beautiful black skin.

White mama, black sons. Deeply demoralized and shaking scared, I keep on fiercely loving them, and wait and hope for the world to see them as I do.

8

WATCHING AND WAITING

Nicole McJamerson

My son is cute. Really, he is—not just because all mamas think their babies are cute, either. I watch people stop, turn around, and admire him. "What a cute little boy!" they say. "Look, how cute he is!" I look, and see his caramel color, with big, bright eyes, and long lashes. He's got his father's ready smile, and boundless energy. What's not to like? It makes me uneasy sometimes, when people talk about how cute he is—especially out here, in the suburbs. Some people like him because he's cute and sweet and smart. But I know that some people are on a timer: they feel comfortable liking him because he's *little*. And one day, he won't be little anymore.

One day when I was pregnant, my specialist told me that my children were small. Even for twins, they were too small, in fact. I watched on the computer screen as the doctor drew a little line across my babies' tummies. As small as my daughter was, my son was even smaller. "Too skinny," he said. I would have to stop work, go home, and sit down. I would have to literally move as little as possible, so that my muscles weren't using up calories that my hungry babies needed. Week after week, I would watch my babies grow: a centimeter here, or there. My daughter grew much faster than my son. I asked the doctor why, and got no real answer. Finally, it got to be such a problem that the kids and I were sent to the hospital. They had to be rescued from my body. When my son was born, we finally saw the problem: the umbilical cord was wrapped around his neck three times. I watch the video of my children's birth from time to time—watch them unwind and unwind the cord. In quiet moments, I am ashamed of this. After all, the womb is the very definition of safety and security. We make fun of people that we deem cowardly by saying they want to *go back to the womb.* But my womb was declared too dangerous for habitation, like a condemned building. I had failed at protecting my children from the very start, in the most basic way possible. How would I ever succeed at protecting them later?

We moved into this specific area of town because of the schools. Before the kids, we moved wherever we liked. Before I got pregnant, my husband and I envisioned raising our kids in an all-Black neighborhood, like the one I grew up in or like the block he grew up on. Sure, it was not without problems, but nobody was scared or mad because some little Black boy was walking down the street. It was safe to go to the gas station and buy candy. It was safe to go to the park. But places like Inglewood, Compton, Hawthorne, and Watts—those places seem to be where the police brutality has become extreme. And there were just a million other reasons not to move to South Central Los Angeles—I've watched the news, and seen all the movies. But the biggest issue was that we simply got priced out. The rents were surprisingly high. The public schools in Los Angeles are troubled, at best. And paying for private school for two kids at one time? That was totally out of the question. Who knew that one could be *too broke* to live in the 'hood? So we moved to the suburbs.

"You have to watch them," my mother nods sagely at my husband and me. "You know how they are." And we do. We know who "they" and "them" are. One day, "they" will be teachers who either don't think my kids can learn, or are surprised by how much they know. Then, "they" will be the folks who are surprised that my kids "play so well" on the playground, or the ones that watch their boys extra carefully when playing with my son. It's easy to identify them at the playground, too: I wait until my son is with a pack of boys. Then, when the pack races past a bench full of mothers, I look for the mother that looks startled when my child runs by. When she sees me or my husband, she usually settles back down, like a flustered hen. That one, I say to myself. That one bears watching. She's one of them.

The thing is, I don't want to be like this. I mean, you are supposed to teach your children they can go anywhere, and do anything. And you're supposed to model how to be a good person, not suspicious and guarded, but open and friendly. "Be the change you want to see in the world," right? Except I can't do that. That's not how it is. Not for my husband, or me, and not for my kids. Being Black in the United States is a weird story of *almost*, and *not quite*. I can teach my kids about how my grandfather was born onto our family's land, which we still own. But someone right now is talking about Americans, and they don't mean me or my family. My kids proudly learned the Pledge of Allegiance, and my son is quick to spot the American flag on houses, books, in front of the post office. But someone who wants to hurt my child, or say hateful things to or about him, is going to hide behind that flag. I will have to teach my son that his beloved flag will not be his shield like it will be for some of his friends. Right now, he loves policemen. He waves to them, and smiles, and gets excited every time we see a police car. I cringe in the front seat, thinking of a time when a police car pulling up behind him will be the stuff of nightmares. One of the little blonde girls in my son's class runs up to us at a party. She has declared in the past that she is going to marry him. "Your son is so cute!" her mom exclaims. "Thank you," I say. "He's a good boy." I wonder if she will still think my son is cute in a few years. Her husband is a police officer. I wonder if he will remember my son, or just jam his knee in my baby's neck like I imagine he does all the other Black men he arrests. We all smile at each other.

All the things that should be celebrated have become more worries. As the smallest one in the house, my son's primary objective right now is Getting Big and Strong. We have convinced him to even eat his vegetables in pursuit of this goal. And yet in this country, every Black child's growth spurt is viewed with suspicion (on some folks' parts) and fear (on my part). Is this the time that he grows too tall to be "little"? Or is too old to be "cute"? What happens when his voice, always husky, finally deepens? What about puberty? We will have to take him to a mirror, and show him that the body he is so proud of growing will become to some a monster that symbolizes everything bad and dangerous and wrong in this country. His strength, his size, his youthful exuberance—all this will be threatening to someone, and danger will follow my son. We must tell him these things. This to me is the cruelest trick of racism: that to be a good parent of a Black child, I should tell my son every day that he is loved—because of who he is. And then I must tell him that he is hated, because of *what* he is. Not only will he be hated, but I have to tell my precious baby that he is considered worthless. How can he be considered otherwise? Black boys get killed, and it's said that it was their fault. Black boys get killed, and their murderers go free—if they're white. Hardly any of them even lose their jobs. And people say to themselves, "that's too bad," while being relieved that the police are just "doing their jobs." If a Black boy's murderer is Black, though—then that person will likely get as much time as the judge can give him due to the precious life he took, as well as general condemnation as a "monster." I marvel sometimes at the math involved in this situation. So far, I have come up with the following equations: One Black boy killed + one Black boy doing the killing = 1 murderous monster − 1 priceless angel, but that same Black boy killed + one White man doing the killing = 1 helpless, defenseless citizen − 1 monster? What does that make the boy who was killed? Is he an angel or a monster? Why aren't these equations equal? It does not compute.

How do we tell my son that he can be killed at a moment's notice? That no one may care, or may only care if he's always a "perfect angel" and an honor-roll student, and is always exactly where he's supposed to be, and nobody thinks he's supposed to be somewhere else. Who inflicts this kind of fear and pain on their sons, except Black people? And what kind of parents are we, if we stop giving our sons these painful, terrible lessons?

My son flings himself around the playground as if it was his personal gym. He swings with abandon, races around on the top, and then almost throws himself down the slides. That is the way he has lived, and I won't stop him. But there are limits to what I can do to protect him right now. I try to see which direction the danger is coming from, but I can't see everything, all the time. And even the things I know are coming, I can't see yet. "Watch me, Mama!" he screams from the jungle gym. "Look at me! Watch me!" I smile and wave. "Your son is just adorable," someone says. "Thank you," I respond. And then I watch him some more.

9

THE TROUBLE I'VE SEEN . . .
AND WHY IT MATTERS

Meta G. Carstarphen

Mr. Martin had been visiting other residents of the complex and had been out that rainy evening to go to a nearby store . . . when Mr. Zimmerman saw him and considered him suspicious.—New York Times, *May 18, 2012*

On a cold, winter night, fuzzy with the drift of a steady snowfall, I stood behind the closed door of my walk-in closet. In the dark. Half-dressed. Shivering.

A quiet and subtle flow of warm air confirmed what I logically knew to be true—my home's heating system still worked. In the dim light, the clothes that surrounded me were vague, indistinctive shapes, lurking like menacing figures had I not known them personally and intimately. Intellectually, I should have felt safe in my own home, but my rapid heartbeats contradicted sound judgment. Caught between fury and confusion, I gingerly turned on the lights and listened to the voices outside my bedroom. Amid the familiar cadences of family members, there seemed to be a new, deeper, unfamiliar intonation. He, so obviously male, was speaking, but I couldn't make out the words.

"Nearly 50 years ago, 14-year-old Emmett Till, a black teen-ager from Chicago, was brutally murdered in rural Mississippi by two white men after he allegedly whistled at a white woman."—All Things Considered (NPR), *January 7, 2003*

In the way that history informs memory, I have tried to make sense of the swell of mediated accounts about violent assaults against men of color by looking to the past. When filmmaker Stanley Nelson released his 2004 documentary *The Murder of Emmett Till*, he privileged the account of Till's mother, Mamie Till-Mobley. Her courage was legend, and with a mother's heart, I relate to her choices. In 1955, she sent her fourteen-year-old son to relatives living in Money, Mississippi, hoping that the warmth of family affection and the presence of male relatives would help the young boy negotiate manhood successfully. After his brutal murder, she displayed her son's savaged body for the world to see, generating international headlines and outrage. She endured a trial where the defenders of her son's killers challenged the entire atrocity based upon an argument that the body returned to her was so unrecognizable that Mamie could not surely be so resolute that this corpse was her son.

Then, in 2012, Sybrina Fulton sent her seventeen-year-old son, Trayvon Martin, to a small Florida community where his father lived. When his murdered body returned to her, I wonder, with a mother's heart, was Trayvon the new Emmett?

My oldest son is grown, college educated, and has worked in the public school system with autistic students. I have, yes, been relieved that he has made it past those teenage years alive. But that was before Eric Garner, John Crawford, and Luis Rodriguez, among others. It was before I found myself in my closet.

"As the two on-duty Moore [Oklahoma] officers were leaving, a person ran into the lobby and told them about some kind of domestic dispute outside. . . . What happened next is disputed. . . . Nair Rodriguez has said officers beat Luis Rodriguez."—CNN, February 26, 2014

"Witness Ronald Ritchie told a 911 dispatcher that Crawford was pointing the gun at children, a claim he repeated to the media. Earlier this month Ritchie changed his story, apparently after viewing the surveillance video."—Washington Post, September 25, 2014

I wanted to wear something special for our New Year's Eve family dinner and activities. I wavered between two outfits when a glaring, white light flooded through our bedroom windows, which face a private pond on our property. I screamed. I heard voices and saw a fleeting body move through the enclosed patio attached to our house, before retreating to the closet.

Was this a joke? Or something more? I quickly dressed, leaving the closet wearing convenient clothes. I no longer cared if the colors matched.

"I'm sorry, ma'am, for startling you," the tall, uniformed officer said to me. He had his hand on another door, backing out towards the patio. There was someone else behind him, who I only saw as a phantom moving towards the outside darkness.

My husband stood next to the recliners where both he and our son had been sitting moments before. Locking his eyes on mine, sensing my fury and confusion, he spoke evenly. There had been a mistake. *No problem.* A woman driving in the opposite lane from our son's car thought she saw the vehicle swerve. It was snowing—a rare event in Oklahoma—and streetlights are rare on country roads. She turned around on the highway and followed his car to our home. She called the police because she was "concerned." An officer came and there we were.

My son was looking puzzled but calm. I focused on my husband's eyes again as he repeated, in a soothing voice, that all was well. My husband handled the goodbyes.

The history of violence against men of color is littered with moments like these, where people I have come to think of as "shadow witnesses" speak with imagination, half-truths, and authority. White privilege enlarges the place of innuendo and suspicion into action and conviction. Shadow witnesses, whose testimony has no real form or substance, might be the start of an honest investigation. But we must not continue, as a society, to give unquestioned weight and authority to such tenuous claims.

"A 12-year-old boy shot by police after grabbing what turned out to be a replica gun died from his wounds Sunday, a day after officers responded to a 911 call about someone waving a 'probably fake' gun at a Cleveland playground."—People Magazine, November 24, 2014

I am grateful, that in my moment, our unnamed officer had the wisdom to discern our truth, to understand that our son was neither a threat, nor a stranger who did not belong to us.

I wish that I could say this incident happened so long ago that it was only a distant memory. But that would be a lie. This was in 2013, less than a year after Trayvon Martin's murder. It was fifty-eight years after Emmett Till's lynching. And, it was less than two months before a family friend, Luis Rodriguez, would be beaten to death by five uniformed security guards, including police officers, as he was leaving a local movie theater. Brown-skinned Luis blended in easily in his native Puerto Rico, but in the Oklahoma landscape, he must have seemed like one, "big, dark threat."

"After Michael Brown was shot dead in August, his mother, Leslie McSpadden, said, 'My son was sweet. He didn't mean any harm to anybody.' He was, she said, 'a gentle giant.' But when police officer Darren Wilson fired the shot that ended Brown's life, he saw things differently. 'I felt like a five-year-old holding onto Hulk Hogan,' he said in his testimony to the grand jury. 'That's just how big he felt and how small I felt.'"—Code Switch (NPR), November 26, 2014

I looked at my son again. I know my testimony about him—his character, his worth, his humanity. My stories must be stronger than the shadows.

"Everything," I repeated, "is fine."

10

INSIDE/OUTSIDE

Susan Hadley

Each time I have attempted to begin these reflections I have felt im-
mobilized because of the multiple aspects of my identity and also those
of my sons. In some ways I felt like an intruder into the book. In some
ways I felt that as a member of the oppressor group, my experiences
were less valid. I am a white Australian woman, married to an African
American man. I have a stepson who is African American and four sons
who are biracial. I have been in my stepson's life since he was six and, as
he was always in the full custody of my husband, I lived with him from
the time he was eleven until he was about twenty. I am mentioning all
of this to say that for the first twenty-five years of my life, I was not
really conscious of what it would entail to be the mother of black sons. I
didn't have to. I didn't have a black father, black brothers or cousins, or
black friends. I was socially conscious and was aware of a multitude of
injustices, but until I became a mother, I had no firsthand experiences.

When I told my liberal, Christian, white parents that I was planning
to get married, I distinctly remember them saying something along the
lines of, "You need to think about the children." My initial response was
anger, knowing full well that they had not said this to my white sister
and her white partner or to my white brother and his Chinese American
partner. I was outraged by their unconscious racism. I felt that, perhaps
in my naïveté, as long as children had parents who loved each other and
loved them, then that was the main thing. While I knew there were a lot
of obstacles and societal pushback to interracial relationships, I was sure
that the depth of love we expressed and experienced would conquer all.

65

I think that the first time I began to feel the weight of being the mother of black sons was when my stepson entered high school. Unfortunately, when I was first thrown into motherhood, he was entering middle school. As a foreigner, I had no understanding of the education system in the United States and did not realize that it would be in his best interest to have him apply to be in the magnet program or even to be tested for the gifted program. As a result, when he reached high school, he was put into the middle tier of students. Having not had a tiered system in elementary or middle school, he had performed at a very high level up until this point. As he reached high school, we noticed that his grades were slipping and he seemed not to have much homework at all. So, we organized to meet with his school counselor. I remember feeling that she did not seem to be concerned about the issues we were raising, commenting that boys will be boys. My gut response was that I was sure she was not saying that to the parents of white boys. I also sensed that there was no investment in him doing well. I felt that they saw limited potential and prospects in him. What made me furious was that they seemed to be suggesting that his problems stemmed from what he was or was not getting at home. I remember several conversations where we were letting her know that we were both academics and that he was living in an environment that valued learning. Again, I wondered whether I would have been made to feel this way if my stepson had been white. Of course, I will never really know the answer to that question. What is profound to me is that if he had been white, that question would never have entered my consciousness.

When my stepson became old enough to stay out late into the night, a new set of concerns became very real to me. I know this happens to parents of late teens of all "races," but this had a new twist for me. When he had not called or come home at a certain time, there were the usual worries of whether or not he had been in a car accident, or whether or not he had been somewhere where there was alcohol or drugs, or whether he might be having unsafe sex. But I began worrying about whether he might have been beaten up by racist whites, whether he was being seen as "up to no good" or in an area "where he shouldn't be" and of all the unthinkable scenarios that could grow out of these perceptions (and this was well before what happened to Trayvon Martin). I remember one night he went from our house to the one across the street to feed the neighbor's dog. Another neighbor was coming home from work, so my stepson said hi. The neighbor (a heavy white male) was so frightened by him that he lost his footing and cried out. Deep inside of me, I believe that his fear was exacerbated by the fact that my stepson is black. Could I be wrong? Yes. But there is so much evidence of implicit bias that a generous reading feels forced.

When my boys were little, strangers would stop us in the street to tell us how beautiful they were. I think this happens a lot to biracial children. When I look at my oldest son, who is now sixteen, I still see that beautiful young innocent child. I knew in theory that others would begin to see him as black and thereby dangerous, but I don't think anything prepares you for the hurt of that reality. He was fairly sheltered growing up, and we talked a lot at home about race from the time that our sons were in preschool. My sixteen-year-old is the most socially conscious of the boys and the most invested in his heritage, spending lots of time gathering as much information about his family tree from both sides. He and I are able to talk freely about almost anything.

One evening, my husband asked me whether my son had told me about his experience that day on the bus. I said that he had not. He then proceeded to tell me that when he had stood up to get off the bus, an older white woman had pulled her possessions closer to her. I was curious as to why he hadn't told me about it because he was very upset by the experience. Later, I told him that I had heard what had happened to him and asked him how he was feeling about it. He said he was really angry about it. He said that he looked her directly in the eyes to see whether she felt any remorse. He could not see any. He said that at first he tried to believe it was because he was a tall teenage male. I asked him whether he believed that was what it was. He said, "No, it was because she saw me as black and therefore as dangerous!" We talked about how if he had been a white male teenager and she had pulled her possessions closer to her, he wouldn't have had to wonder whether or not it was because of his racialized identity. He went on to say that we had always explained that this is how he would be seen, no matter how light skinned he is. He said that although he never believed that we were deceiving him, it did not really sink in until that moment.

This moment on the bus hurt my son to his core. He has black and white family, black and white friends, and sees himself as a mixture of both, as a kind of symbol of the possibility of that harmony between the two. But at the moment this white woman pulled her bag closer to her body, violence had taken place. What might be perceived as a micro aggression has had a macro impact. My son now knows from firsthand experience that he is perceived as a threat, and he has to carry that with him for the rest of his life. And as a mother, I am powerless to do anything about the pain that he has to bear. I can't do shit! And in the back of my head I hear, "But what about the children. . . . You need to think about the children." No amount of love can protect them from these experiences.

I then began to think about how these experiences inform how each of us as parents can relate to him. His father has those same firsthand experiences and can resonate with how he feels. I, on the other hand, in many ways, represent the white woman on the bus. Perhaps that could have been me. Have I done this to a black male at some point in my life? Have I seen him as a threat and not as a vulnerable human being? When he looked into the eyes of that white woman, he wanted to see reflected back the recognition of *his* humanity. Instead, he felt disappointment that she had this knee-jerk reaction. I think he wanted to see family. But he didn't and so he had to face a truth he had been resisting.

My second eldest son is fifteen. He is our phenotypically darkest son and also at this point the son who most likes to resist authority—the most hotheaded—at home and at school. When I get calls from the school, I wonder how his behaviors are being filtered through the lens of race. Our kids have all come home at some point asking why it is that more African American children are sent to the office than white kids. This son is not as conscious about world events as his older brother. Yet he is just as vulnerable.

As we were preparing for one of our trips to Australia, this son commented that there is no one there who looks like him. While I assured him that this was not the case, I did say that he is right that where my family lives, there are mostly white people. It reminded me of a time when he commented that he and his father were the only two black people living on our street (ironically not seeing his brothers as also black). These instances indicate an awareness that is often not acknowledged by him. When we were in Australia, we visited my parents' church with them. This same son heard a young white girl say, "I've never played with a black child before." At that moment he was marked in a way he had not felt before. Like with the experience with our older son, he went to talk with his dad about it. He wasn't just different because he was from the United States, but he was distinguished by his skin color. While she said it with excitement, he had to wonder why she had not experienced this before. I mean, just how segregated are white Australian children? Thinking back, I had a few Chinese, Japanese, and Indian friends, but no African friends. I knew a couple of Aboriginal children, but not many.

I worry about my fifteen-year-old son every day. I worry that if he is harassed or confronted, he will fight back. We want our children to stand up for themselves and not be pushed around, but we also want them to stay alive. It seemed so surreal for me to have a conversation with a fifteen-year-old, going step-by-step through what to do and what not to do if he is ever stopped by police. My parents never had these conversations with my brothers, and they were much "wilder" than my sons, engaging in much riskier behaviors. When I was telling him what he needed to do, he protested, saying that police wouldn't do bad things to you. How do you explain to a kid who gets the opposite messages about police officers from books, movies, and teachers that, yes, they can do bad things to you and often do? Hearing example after example, he just shook his head and said that those are just bad cops, and they will get in trouble for that. But so often they don't.

It is easy for children and white people to see each instance of racist violence *as an exception* to the rule. It is much easier to do this than to take in the systemic nature of racism. If we keep looking at each case as an aberration, we do not need to look at the depth of its reach. We do not need to look at ourselves (in my case) or at our family and friends (in my case and in the case of my children). We can get outraged anew at each case, rather than seeing it *as the rule*, with the lack of racist violence as the exception. But the older my boys get, and the more cases of racist violence towards African Americans by white police and white civilians come into the public view, the more the fear mounts in me. What if they are next? How can I protect them? How do I encourage them to live fulfilling and happy lives, and yet arm them with a healthy amount of fear, suspicion, and courage? How do I raise them as Christian and yet ask them not to have faith? How do I teach them to love and yet keep their eyes open to the horrors of humanity? It feels so different from how I was raised. But to not find this balance is to send them into the world unprepared, unprotected. To shelter me from these realities growing up was not to put my future possibilities at risk.

When Trayvon Martin was killed, President Obama commented that if he had a son, he would have looked like Trayvon Martin. Well, I do have sons (five of them). One may look a little like Trayvon, the others, not so much. But it doesn't matter. To live in a space where we are continually reminded that Black Lives Don't Matter—Amadou Diallo, Oscar Grant, Trayvon Martin, Jordan Davis, Jonathan Ferrell, Ranisha McBride, Eric Garner, Rumain Brisbon, Anthony Hill, Tamir Rice, Walter Scott, Eric Harris, Alton Sterling, Philando Castile—the one-drop rule still applies and the weight of racial profiling and violence continues to haunt my (and other mothers') sons.

11

BLACK AND BLUE

Stressing through to Dialogue

Deborah Binkley-Jackson

I am: the wife of a thirty-year career police officer; a Black woman who holds an undergraduate degree in law enforcement administration; and, a loving mother of a Black son (and daughter). I am, far too often afraid. There are other personal attributes that I consider important and critically relevant to who I feel I am as a person. However, for the moment, I am plagued with anxieties produced by those identity markers I have just mentioned.

President Barack Obama, on July 19, 2013, verbalized during his initial comments following the murder of Trayvon Martin "that this could have been my son."[1] I understood that statement. The fact of the matter is that President Obama's statement, and the sentiment behind it, had also been thought and verbally expressed by many people I knew. It permeated my own thoughts immediately upon hearing about Trayvon's death, and for several days following. It lingered throughout the trial and the aftermath of the verdict; indeed, such thoughts have continued nearly every day since. Unremarkably, President Obama's statement continues to fill my home as my husband and I talk with our daughter and son, but mainly our son, about the reminders. To be more specific, we talk about the "codes of conduct" that he is to assume during his various day-to-day experiences in the country in which we live. These conversations include: never putting your hands in your pockets when you are in a store; getting a receipt for everything you purchase; keeping your hands on the steering wheel if you are stopped by a police officer until he or she instructs you to do otherwise; answering only the specific questions asked of you; being aware of the reputations of the people you have riding in your car or with whom you are riding. Discussion with many of my White friends and colleagues have shed light that these conversations inclusive of "codes" are not prevalent in their homes.

As the wife of a Black police officer, I understand, at a very intimate level, the dangers associated with this profession. I firmly believe, however, that there are more inherently good people in the world. I propose that with every civilian contact, no matter where, an officer has a 50 percent chance of meeting someone who wants to cause him or her, or the public at large, no harm. Regarding the other 50 percent, I propose that an officer will come into contact with someone who will initiate actions that pose a threat to police officers, or the public at large. I am reminded of a quote attributed to Albert Einstein that says, "One cannot simultaneously prevent and prepare for war."[2] The stress of constantly having to be in a state of wanting to expect the best but also having to prepare for the worst is taxing on the mind, the body, and the spirit. I have conversed with a number of Black men who have been stopped for nothing more than DWB (driving while Black). More than their white counterparts, they have been stopped and questioned. They have been issued a citation or allowed to go on their way without having been provided with any explanation as to why they were stopped other than satisfying the inquisition of the officer.

My hope is that the tragic deaths of too many of our Black males will not be in vain. My hope is that the law enforcement community will understand the winds of change that have come about because this country has grieved enough from losing our Black sons. My hope is that the law enforcement community will genuinely recognize the racist stereotypes attributed to Black people, and, more specifically, Black males. Such racist stereotypes perpetuate the view that our Black men/boys have a propensity for emotionally charged violence and lawlessness. Such racist stereotypes far too often manifest themselves on the streets as "truth" wrapped in a police clad uniform with weaponry to boot. In many American communities, diversity sensitivity and awareness training with law enforcement agencies is often minimal, trivialized, or totally nonexistent. Most municipalities that do include diversity training as part of their cadet curriculum do not require continuing education criteria and training as a standardized component in maintaining police officer qualifications. There is clearly a difference of mindset between the general public and the law enforcement community about how recognizing and confronting the societal ills of all forms of prejudice should be addressed.

I too am proud of my husband and of the exemplary job he has performed in a highly stressful and dangerous profession. He too is a Black mother's son. I know that there are other police officers, Black and white, across our nation, who work with high levels of ethical integrity and who have profound respect for human life. I am also fully and painfully aware that there are law enforcement personnel who carry personal baggage, along with their arsenal of weaponry, onto the streets of America every day. They are filled with prejudices, misplaced fears, and racist stereotypes. These are the officers who challenge my desire to control the fear that one day they will be the ones who will target my son, my father, my nephews, and my cousins.

If there are parts of this essay that appear disparate or incongruent, then welcome to my world. I have empathy, both when it comes to recognizing the tasks that our law enforcement communities have been charged with and when it comes to recognizing the disenfranchised plight of Black males that exists within too many of our nation's communities. The Black and blue in my home are blended and blurred. However, what is crystal clear to me is that perpetuating an atmosphere where poisoned bitterness between law enforcement and non–law enforcement groups continues to perpetuate negative stereotypes about each other cannot be the legacy we want to leave our children. Without respectful dialogue that incorporates active listening, empathy, and a concern to move beyond stalemates, protests, riots, entrenched fraternal silence, defensiveness, and protectiveness, our nationwide communities will not be able to bridge the divide that threatens to cause more civic and bodily harm than help to Black men.

Dialogue is hard work. There will be those who want, even need, to hold onto the grief and anger that is typically felt when a life is taken needlessly. The emotions that often accompany the loss of a loved one due to violence is hard to look at and even harder to digest. Making collective discourse even more difficult is the fact that we are not a nation that likes to spend time dwelling on the racial and ethnic disparities that have existed, and continue to exist, in our country since Africans were forcibly brought to this country to be systematically thrown into the institution of slavery. Not to be excluded is the harsh reality of white privilege that was once sanctioned by laws and remains as a reality of de facto institutionalized racism that still tends to one-sidedly tip the scales of "justice."

If future conversations cannot be critical and inclusive of multiple perspectives, we will fail as a nation to grapple successfully with the problem of police brutality and the deaths of so many Black men/boys. If we don't challenge the ways that stereotypes have helped to shape fears, actions, and reactions, then we will patronize Blacks, placate our judicial system, and fail to save lives. We are an impatient society, and dialogue takes time, but it is a manageable challenge and a space within which the miracle of peace can be found. Otherwise, we may all go down in flames together.

12

A BLACK JEWISH BOY
FACING MANHOOD

Jane Anna Gordon

When my son had finished all of his responsibilities for the day—he had been wrapped by his grandfather in the tallit, had lifted the Torah from the ark, had carried it through the assembled singing community, had undressed it, blessed it, chanted from it, interpreted the significance of the ancient phrases he'd uttered, then re-cloaked and returned it safely—it was my husband and my turn to bless our beloved son, the Bar Mitzvah. Relishing the opportunity to speak candidly and publicly about Elijah, I had woken up early that morning thinking through the specific words I wanted to say. Part of the blessing went like this:

You, Elijah, do not have a conformist bone in your body or a conforming sinew in your flesh: what motivates and excites you; what you fear and what you loathe—they are all very distinct. You are motivated by values and concerns that really are your own.
   There are so many examples:

   One is the way that, for you, Halloween was the holiday when you found a scarily real (which is ironic) unicorn mask and decided that you wanted to be the unicorn of West Hartford. You would don the mask to go to Stop n' Shop or school—to any place that would let you—delighting in the idea of all of these ordinary places having a mythic creature moving through them!

Or the way, when taking many very long drives, you would ask your older sisters, Jenni and Sula, to call you "Eliza" so you could play on the fact that many people confused your pretty face for a girl's, enabling you to use the cleaner women's bathrooms—and this at a time when many of your friends were doing everything to make sure that EVERY-ONE knew AT ALL TIMES that they were male.

Or the way that you chose to wear your hair like Samson the Nazar-ite—even as some people thought it was strange or ugly.

Or the fact that you are so strongly black identified when you could very easily move through the world as a young white man.

May you continue to have the chutzpah to live with the creativity that you do.

Against the grain of much of the multiracial politics that dominated the 1990s, my husband and I took the position that even children who are now often called "biracial," tend to be healthier college students and adults if they simply call and think of themselves as *black*. This does not mean hiding the full complexity of who they are—Elijah, while begin-ning with his Jamaican-ness, will as comfortably tell you that he is Jew-ish and Irish and Tamil and Chinese and Palestinian and Lithuanian. For all my arguments otherwise, he swallows when he also admits that he is German.

The reasons for the insistence on the primary quality of their black-ness are multiple: First, as my husband always repeats, modern black-ness has always been a mixed category. He will regularly ask the kids to describe the (vast) color spectrum of people who would gather at one of his mother's many parties in the Bronx. (Among them were always "black" people as light as their "white" mother.) As I realized so palpa-bly by contrast when first visiting Dakar, Senegal, there is no such thing as American non-mixed black people. At issue is simply with what other non-African groups they are mixed. All of this is to say that *it is the category "white" that aims to exclude all mixture, that seeks purity to sustain itself as white, and so affixing "mixed" to "New World black" is redundant and misleading (in suggesting that a rule is an exception).*

Second, while many popular biracial narratives suggest otherwise, few black children with a white parent are treated in the same way by the families of both parents. In part because of the first point about blackness always being a mixed category while whiteness aims at purity, black communities have historically been the haven and refuge for the couples and children turned away by others. While this may be in part a function of what it is to lack the powers to exclude, it is also a distinct and powerful virtue, an ethic that surely should be recognized, admired, and emulated.

Third, and linked to the prior two points, part of being exclusive is preserving the ways of thinking that rationalize exclusionary choices as necessary and legitimate. In effect, this requires the bad faith of enshrouding oneself in pleasing falsehoods that lubricate the motions of daily life; making decisions that open up opportunities for some by closing them off to others appears as an unintended, distant outcome. It is not that black communities are without self-deceptions, but they are rarely those linked to maintaining a monopoly on power.

None of this is to say that my son Elijah has nothing to do with his maternal family. Quite the opposite. It does mean that those dimensions of them that he prizes most are not "white," but tied instead to the ethno-cultural aspects of who we are. I tell him often about the socialist Zionism of my grandmother who hoped that an egalitarian utopia might be built in the mid-twentieth-century Middle East. We joke about the thickness of his calves as legacies of eastern European peasants. Or, with my daughter, I will discuss the proto-feminism of her German great-aunts who were educators experimenting with early environmentalism. We wonder about the "German" source of their rich brown skin and thick dark curls.

While I am very aware of the frustration caused when people who move through the social, political, and economic world as *white* stress their ethnic dimensions—this seems to downplay the decisive significance of their racial standing; the pivotal ways that they are placed by others—I did always understand the historical meaning of being Jewish as fundamentally troubling what it meant to be white. Not only was there the recent past of Jews not being considered fully European, a fact that should have led all Jews, regardless of their phenotype, to question any allegiance to identity categories tied to the project of Europe. Jews were, even before that, a colonized and dispersed people, fundamentally shaped by the experience of being exiles and strangers. If belonging anywhere, Jews did so with a precariousness that meant that we had a special obligation to others facing similar circumstances. When my family moved to South Africa and then to England and then to the United States, it was Jewishness (within a British Empire) that made sense of these migratory patterns. Regardless of what one felt about religious observance, the imperative communicated to me was that I, as a Jew, was to live this history meaningfully in the present.

It was for this reason that I also was instantly persuaded by James Baldwin's essay that so many disliked, "Blacks Are Anti-Semitic Because They Are Anti-White." It challenged European Jews (Baldwin did not address black Jews because they did not enter this equation as white; their blackness trumped their religious heritage) to recognize that they did not occupy the same historic political location on this side of the Atlantic; in the United States a "new serf" had been created—the black person—and it was understanding his or her situation that was essential here.

When I told my teenage children that I'd enthusiastically accepted an invitation to write about mothering black sons, trying not to be disrespectful, they wanted to know why. As my daughter put it, "Elijah is so light-skinned, white people often think he is white. He is not facing the possibility of being another Eric Garner." Elijah also, while very wary of "the pigs," figured that unlike his older brother, with him we are spared many reasons to fear.

I thought that this was exactly the point: Elijah, the youngest and lightest skinned of four siblings, had always been very close to our eldest, my stepson, his dark-skinned brother for whom, in part because of his six-foot-two, 350-pound stature, and in part because of his extreme social anxiety, it only seemed a matter of time before he had some dangerous run-in with law enforcement. The basicness of this difference does determine how they negotiate the U.S. social landscape in ways that Elijah's black identification only mildly mediates.

Elijah *is* often singled out from other kids by insecure figures of authority, but more for seeming anomalous—for being hard to place in ways that race and racism, gender, sexism, and heterosexism are supposed to eliminate. This could as easily be accounted for by his appearing much older than his peers; his standing a full foot taller; his looking, to them, as if he were disheveled in self-presentation due, in part, to his effort to embody his black Jewishness (the basis for his nickname "Six Dreads").

The scene is repeated so frequently in dramatic presentations of black life because of its ubiquity beyond the screen and printed page. I saw it most recently in Denzel Washington's 2007 *The Great Debaters*, which takes place in the United States of the 1930s: Dr. James Farmer Sr., the president of Wiley College Texas (played by Forest Whitaker), who demands that his children meet the most exacting of intellectual and behavioral standards as an expression of their dignity, is out one day with his family when a hog runs into the road. Although he slams on the brakes, the car slides and hits the animal. Two white farmers, pink, sweaty, and dirty—uneducated and not in control of their land—corner Dr. Farmer, speaking to him threateningly and demanding that he pay a massively inflated price for their now-dead pig. Dr. Farmer's family looks on, horrified and scared, seeing their father enact the forced choice between being shot down for standing up or performing the role of the cowering Negro on demand.

While Elijah has had the good fortune of repeatedly watching his father refuse this forced choice, even when doing so involves conflict and temporary losses, there is a general lesson that more fully entering a black world through marriage and parenting has taught me: one must live as if values and virtues and excelling and being a person of integrity matter, *for that is what it is to live a human life*. At the same time, one has to know in equal measure that the whole point of antiblack racism is that to distinguish oneself as a black person in these or any other ways matters externally only if the person encountering you is secure or idealistic enough to care. When this is not the case, these distinctions are probably a liability. In other words, I now better understand the noble dignity of so many black Africans and Americans that struck me as a child. Exhibited proudly, it is embodied in spite of the dangers; in reference to an existing world in which whiteness recedes and one to come in which it is made irrelevant; it seems to beckon, "bring it on!"

As is so frequently the case, the treatment of black life offers a unique mirror into the political present. What we are witnessing in U.S. cities—the desire of police to free their work of *any* risk by placing all of it on anyone who they fear might endanger them; their demand to be accountable to no rules, not even those of their profession; their want to *be* the law in whichever way they think it should be enunciated—in the recent spate of unapologetic antiblack killings is also evident in the global rise of instances of literal enslavement, situations of radical unfreedom through which unilateral relations are curbed neither by law nor political mechanisms. Fighting against normalizing such circumstances is essential both so that black and brown boys and men live as something other than disposable and, relatedly, as an expression of our refusal to abandon the project of developing a domain of political life that is not, as laws of physics, dominated entirely by those with more force and its economic counterpart, capital.

This ongoing fight is an expression of what it is to be, as Elijah, a black Jew.

II

Essays

13

SACRIFICIAL LAMBS

How Many Dead Bodies Is Enough?

Carol E. Henderson

In the hills, a voice is heard, crying and weeping loudly. Rachel mourns for her children and refuses to be comforted, because they are dead.—Jeremiah 31:15

We bury and mourn the sons who are dead. What will we do to cherish and save the ones who live?—Marita Golden, *Saving Our Sons*

How many a week, how many repetitions of the same sad ceremony must there be?—John Edgar Wideman, "The Killing of Black Boys"

I have *struggled* to write this piece. At first, I thought it was writer's block. Our busy lives as academics, mothers, wives, sisters, friends, community advocates, mentors, teachers, administrators, siblings, daughters, aunts—all of these separate yet intertwining identities can tug at our spirits in challenging and rewarding ways. But it can be exhausting. There are only so many hours in a day . . . so many days in a week. I thought, I need to carve out more time to find a quiet space where I can block out the demands of everyday life and get in tune with the spiritual well of my creativity. There I will find the requisite grace and energy to pen the necessary missive that would speak truth to power, that would *demand* that justice be served on behalf of our young Black men and fathers who have been murdered in the name of the law.

But the words would not come. It was as if I was afraid to utter the horror I have seen, as if not committing it to paper would not make it real. This foreboding truth seemed to haunt my pages. I couldn't wrap my mind around it. What was disturbing me so much that it would not let words on my tongue flow to the tip of my fingers? How come words did not come as easily as they had for other reflections on the troubling and perplexing experiences of our black men in *this* country? This country. The land of the free. The nation where we hold these truths to be *self-evident*, that *all* men are created equal, that they are endowed by their Creator with certain unalienable rights, those being life, liberty, and the privilege to pursue happiness in whatever form that looks like for them. This country. The country where my father and mother created opportunities for me to thrive as a human being; the land where my maternal grandparents raised thirteen children on a pauper's salary to be productive and law abiding citizens—where we were taught to respect everyone, live in harmony with the world—and always hope for the best. This was the country where we were taught that the glass is always half full and the half-empty portion meant there was opportunity for growth to work toward the promise of a better tomorrow. This is the tomorrow I would direct my beautiful man-child to seek, for it was there that he would find the centers of himself, wrapped in the cloak of an ancestral warmth that would embrace him as the regal prince of promise he is destined to be.

But this writer's block was different. It was peppered with the realization that any day on the news I could see a black man shot in the back, killed for driving a car with a broken taillight. Where I could see a father choked to death before my very eyes for selling loose cigarettes. Where a black man could be shot to death in the stairwell to his apartment complex because some police officer was startled by noise in a neighborhood he should know. Where a twelve-year-old child can be killed in front of his fourteen-year-old sister two minutes after the police arrived on the scene. Where walking through your *own* neighborhood wearing a hoodie or playing loud music in the parking lot of a gas station can have you methodically assassinated. Hope seemed to be dwarfed in the face of these murders. A shocking series of murders that is being repeated with a frequency that is beyond alarming—it is terrifying. Terror would turn to anger—rage—then a profound sadness that would have me ask myself, why does it matter that I write *this* piece? What are words on a page going to do for the mother of Tamir Rice? For the mother—the wife and children—of Eric Garner? For the mothers of Trayvon Martin? Michael Brown? Jordan Davis? Ramarley Graham? How can words build a bridge that fills the gulf between their reality and our nightmare?

This primal recognition of black male pain—and the pain of the women who love our black men as husbands and brothers—and birth them as sons—is the haunting echo we hear in the cultural memory of African American people. We know the roll call: Emmett Till. The Atlanta Child Murders. Michael Donald. James Byrd. And now we add Trayvon Martin. Jordan Davis. Tamir Rice. Michael Brown, and a list of names too numerous to include here. *This is the moral crises we are facing*. And more chilling is John Edgar Wideman's evaluation that the killing of our black boys is "an effort to murder our future."[1] And so we black mothers (and fathers) who must live each day with the wearisome inequities of life and death, an imbalance unfair in its laser-like focus on our children—we continue to press our way each day, preserving the good in our children.

And so I know now why I *must* write. I write because writing is fighting, as Ishmael Reed declared many years ago, a way to box your way through the stilted consciousness of bigotry, social injustice, and indifference on paper.[2] I write for my living son who is the joy of my life, and the gift that was bestowed to me by the Creator so that I can pour all that is good in me into him so that he can impact the world in meaningful and purposeful ways. I write to acknowledge that I sometimes wander into that chasm of angst and hope, a rim of possibility that says the world *will* make room for my son to share the wonderful gifts and treasures born in him despite what I see. In teaching our sons to be the best men that they can be, we hope to honor the memories of sons lost.

I write out of a sense of obligation for other black mothers and mothers of black boys who also struggle to cover their sons in hope when the world has sent them a sad and sorry story about their lives and the ways we value them. I write because I want the mothers who have lost their sons to know that our spirits weep with you. We hear your wailing in our collective spirit—a wailing we know will not quiet until justice and just-ness is served. Your sons are our sacrificial lambs; their blood is painted on the doorposts of our homes . . . the homes of us who have living sons. We must speak your sons' names so that their sacrifice is not lost in the public discourse that seeks to dehumanize them, criminalize them in ways to justify the behavior of those who murder them. The overwhelming recognition that these acts of terrorism from eras long past have returned to America's public stage with a vengeance—a vengeance that says, "Black lives are expendable, can disappear, click, just like that, without a trace, so it seems almost as if the son or sister were hardly here at all and maybe Black people really ain't worth s—t just like you've been hearing your whole sorry life"[3] —is grievous to us. We meet this recognition with a dogged determination that says BLACK LIVES MATTER, ALL HUMAN LIFE MATTERS, and we will not be moved to fear and despair.

AND WE WILL CONTINUE TO HOPE. As Nelson Mandela reminds us, "there were many dark moments when [one's] faith in humanity [is] sorely tested, but [he] would not give in to despair. That way lies defeat and death."[4] And so we push on . . . wounded, disillusioned . . . discouraged . . . and sometimes broken. But we move on nonetheless, reminding ourselves of the cost of justice, just-ness, and silence. "Your silence will not protect you,"[5] writes Audre Lorde. And so we speak their names, we remember our children gone too soon, whose spirits encourage us not to forget them . . . and to love the children still among the living. This is the highest honor we can pay to the fallen. *To remind us all that dying will not be our living legacy.* We are a great and mighty people. We will live—our sons will live. They *must* live. This is the true measure of our worth as human beings.

14

REFLECTIONS OF BLACK MOTHERHOOD
Birthing Black Sons

Linda D. Tomlinson

Though the colored man is no longer subject to be bought and sold, he is still surrounded by an adverse sentiment which fetters all his movements. In his downward course he meets with no resistance, but his course upward is resented and resisted at every step of his progress. If he comes in ignorance, rags, and wretchedness, he conforms to the popular belief of his character, and in that character he is welcome. But if he shall come as a gentleman, a scholar, and a statesman, he is hailed as a contradiction to the national faith concerning his race, and his coming is resented as impudence. In the one case he may provoke contempt and derision, but in the other he is an affront to pride, and provokes malice. Let him do what he will, there is at present, therefore, no escape for him. The color line meets him everywhere, and in a measure shuts him out from all respectable and profitable trades and callings. In spite of all your religion and laws he is a rejected man.[1] —Frederick Douglass

At the age of twelve, I remember adamantly saying to my mother and grandmother that I wanted to have a hysterectomy! Did I know what a hysterectomy was? Yes, I did. My mother was a registered nurse and talked about her work on many occasions. I also knew that I did not want to have children, and this was a procedure that would prevent that. Why did I not want children? Well, it had nothing to do with being afraid of what birth would do to my body, the pain childbirth would

surely bring, or the responsibility of raising children. It had everything
to do with growing up a black girl in rural Terrell, Texas, in the 1970s,
just a spit's throw away in time from the full-blown Jim Crow era! When
you hear the advertisement that "Texas is like a whole other country,"
there are vagaries of truth in that statement! Things are a whole lot
bigger in the Lone Star State and the ramifications more profound!

My grandmother, great aunts, and other elderly black folk told us
children about the lynching activities that took place in East Texas
under the cloak of darkness and guise that some black person "stepped
out" of his or her place. What exactly was my place as a black child?
This sense of "place" confused me immensely when I was younger. I
witnessed firsthand the treatment that little black children, like myself,
siblings, and cousins experienced when going into the mom-and-pop
store within walking distance of my grandmother's home and land. We
literally had to beg my grandmother to allow us to go with my Uncle
Dick on his check day to get penny cookies from Mrs. Peale's store. It
was not until I was an adult and a historian that I understood my
grandmother's (who lived through the horrors of Jim Crow Texas) desire to shield us from the disdainful stares and utter disrespect we
received each time we walked into that store and spent my uncle's hard-
earned money. It didn't matter that the white lady was impatient when
we were attempting to make our choices (as my uncle allowed us to do)
or that she threw the cookies back at us as if we were dogs of some kind.
We were kids and all that mattered to us was getting our mouths on
those cookies. Black children have been trying to enjoy cookies and life
for a long time in the United States, which has proven to be very
difficult at various junctures of history.

As I grew older, I began to realize just what it meant to be black in
the United States, especially in the southern part. There are some
things that cannot be changed. Unconsciously, I began to develop survival skills and to deal with the cards life had dealt me. However, I also
began to think seriously about bringing other "black" children into this
world. There are some things that one can change. I was a natural
nurturer, always doing whatever was necessary to protect my brother
and sister. As the oldest sibling, it became my duty to shield them from
the bullies, the unkind words and deeds that sometimes come within
any community. But our community, our world, was segregated and, up
to the seventh grade, so was my education.

The 1970s was a period of experimental change: desegregation, integration, and bussing. Therefore, when school desegregation was mandated in Terrell, Texas, the nurturer found herself facing a whole host of new challenges from which her siblings had to be protected! If segregation and Jim Crow codified white America's separation from black folks, the mandated and managed desegregation brought their vitriolic hatred for blacks to the surface like a festering sore. Everything was about proving yourself capable, fighting to survive and trying to remain humane at the same time. For me, it required an immense amount of energy just to be black. This is not something you want to pass on to your children. This is why as an early teen, I decided that having surgery to prevent motherhood would be the best course for me as a black girl.

Needless to say, my mother and grandmother opposed my decision. They believed I was too young and too immature to make such a profound life-altering decision. In all fairness, their assessment was correct in regard to my immaturity, but deep down I knew the fear that gripped me in terms of what life would hold for my children. I had that fear then and I have it now.

I am the daughter of a black man, the wife of a black man, gave birth to two black sons, and have one black grandson. As a mother of black sons, it is particularly disconcerting to witness what seems to be a new, yet familiar, and daily phenomenon of disregard for black males' lives. Of course, I worry about how the police will respond to my husband, my father, my brothers, my sons, and my grandson if they encounter them in any scenario or situation. As a historian, I am even more concerned because I know the history of black people in this country. I fully understand that black people were considered chattel for centuries. Once freedom came, they were still relegated to a second-class position and as "immature children" to be told what to do. Respect for black life in this country has evaded the national psyche of this country and has influenced how black people navigate through it. Whether we want to admit it or not, black people operate in a survival mode, consciously and unconsciously. Survival mode colored my parenting and continues to influence my experiences as a grandmother.

Naturally, parents want their children's lives to be better than their own. We want our children to experience things we couldn't, break down barriers we couldn't, and achieve accomplishments that we couldn't achieve in our own lives. Always, my main concern and desire for my sons was that they were allowed to live beyond twenty-five years of age. I can honestly admit to this because change in this country will not happen until we face the truth of the matter. Many black women worry that their black boys will not live to see their own twenty-fifth birthday. Yes, I wanted them to be educated, to do well in sports (if they chose that course), and to fall in love and have happy productive lives. Unfortunately, all of those wishes took a back seat to their just staying alive! My prayers at night for them are for God to keep them alive. In essence, I am pleading with God to allow other people to acknowledge their humanity, their worthiness, and their right to life, liberty, and the pursuit of happiness. For me, as a mother, keeping them alive is the most important aspect of my parenting responsibility. I strongly believe in the biblical adage: "While there is life there is hope."[2] Notwithstanding the continued racism, discrimination, and abuses heaped on black people, if my sons are alive, they can struggle against racial profiling, against negation of their humanity, and for the right to a thriving life.

There is a saying in the African American community that black mothers raise their daughters and baby their sons. I could not afford to baby and shield my sons in America where their raced identity is an ever-present liability. I had to raise them in a survival mode, explaining to them the history of racism in this country and the lack of respect for their black bodies and that they might not be allowed to make some of the same ridiculous mistakes of childhood that other groups make without penalty of death.

Being a black male child in the United States doesn't always connote a happy-go-lucky childhood. For example, when in elementary school, my oldest son was attacked by a young, white bigot on his way home from school. The individual threw a rock out of a moving car window and hit my son on his ankle, cracking it. Can you image getting a call at work that someone hit your child, cracking his ankle, on his way from school? Had that rock hit his head, the incident would have been totally different, perhaps even fatal. Not only did I have to explain why someone would do this (which I really couldn't explain adequately), but I also had to tell him to be on guard for such things in the future because his pigmentation was not going to change. You know what he said to me? "Mama, maybe people will change." Unfortunately, I couldn't fathom the mindset of America changing in my lifetime because of the slow pace of change attested to by history (slavery, Jim Crow, etc.). I was a mother who wanted to say to the world, "my boy has a right to try to be something—can you let him?" The fear in my heart for my son's prospects was transforming into anger. This anger wanted and needed an outlet. That outlet became my linear survival parenting. This type of parenting leaves no room for deviation or for my sons to question the legitimacy of such a militaristic regimen. It was as if I became a drill sergeant preparing soldiers for confrontation with the outside world. A confrontation where failure was not an option—they had to win. They had to stay alive.

I tried to make sure that my sons had "positive" male and female role models in their lives, people who were not so jaded that they couldn't inspire my sons to aspire to greater things than mere survival. My ability to do this was almost null and void because the linear survival parenting mode absorbed all of my mothering skills. This is a challenge of black motherhood—to avoid being linear in one's parenting. Unfortunately, I became linear in my parenting because of my past experiences with Jim Crow and racism. Because I couldn't break out of that pattern, other family members, friends, and professionals became the mentors my sons needed in order to thrive. Credit has to be ascribed to God for opening my heart to allow these individuals to complement my survival preparation.

With God's help, as a black woman, I had managed to forge through the quagmire of discrimination and racism that existed in my personal life. Albeit I never feared for my life the way I feared for my sons' lives. I cannot explain this because black women have been and are also subjected to indiscriminate abuse and killings just as black men. It just seems as if the very presence of a black male body in society sends the police and others in power into paroxysms of fear and condemnation. Black women's presence is not feared as abjectly until we speak. Although my color is a problem, it is my mind and voice that are even more problematic in a racist society. Whereas the black male's body is the main catalyst of fear and elicits an aggressive/negative response from much of white America. This knowledge is what drove me as a black woman, raising black boys in a southern state, to engage in the linear survival parenting style.

The mantra "Black Lives Matter" has long been in the hearts, psyches, and souls of black mothers in the United States of America regardless of economic status, education, religion, and political beliefs. In light of the trajectories of Amadou Diallo, Trayvon Martin, Michael Brown, Sean Bell, Walter Scott, Eric Garner, Tamir Rice, Ramarley Graham, and Freddie Gray, once again the light has been shone on the sheer disregard, disrespect, and contempt for black life. Malcolm X reminded America in 1963 that if the nation had respect for the human rights of the African person, there would be no need to beg for civil rights. Does America have respect for the human rights of black people today? Human rights mean that one has a God-given right to exist without threat to his or her person. In Cleveland, Ohio, in 2012, thirteen officers fearing the sound of a car backfiring, fired a total of 137 rounds into a car of an unarmed black couple (Timothy Russell and Melissa Williams), killing them. Of the thirteen officers, one was charged and acquitted. For many black Americans, this indicates and reinforces the fact that there is still no respect of the human rights of black people in our contemporary moment.

On their fifteenth birthdays respectively, I presented both sons with Langston Hughes's poem, "Mother to Son," explaining life had not been easy for me as a black woman. Adding that for them it would be infinitely harder as black men. My prayer and wish for them was simply to "live." Live despite the fact that others in America want you dead.

15

THE WAR WITHIN

Respect and the Predicament of Mothering Black Sons

Newtona (Tina) Johnson

This essay is my attempt as a mother of a Black son and as a feminist scholar to make sense of my angst over mothering Black males in America. I know I am not alone in my maternal trepidation, for weaved through many conversations with other mothers raising Black males are fibers of fear, frustration, pain, and guilt. Given my maternal distress, particularly in this era of what seems like the wanton killing of Black males, I can identify with Michelle Maltais's ambivalence about bringing a Black male child into the world. With courage and pain, Maltais reveals that the announcement that she was going to have a boy simultaneously filled her heart with joy and terror, terror because her adorable baby boy will one day become a "black man."[1] As I read Maltais's revelation and considered my experiences and those of many mothers I know raising Black children, the word *respect* seems to loom large. This essay, therefore, is about respect.

Respect is a multivalent term used with different inflections in colloquial usage and across academic discourses. I do not use the term to mean respectability as in "respectability politics," which Michelle Smith presents as the way in which marginalized classes seek social and political equality by showing that they can be compatible with the mainstream society.[2] I do not espouse the view, to borrow Smith's analogy, that to be respected, Black sons must take off their hoodies and pull up their saggy pants. The sense in which I use the term in this essay is captured well by Stephen J. Pope's concept of *basic respect*. Using as a springboard Immanuel Kant's notion that respect, *Achtung*, should be accorded all rational persons, simply put, Pope conceives of basic respect as the endowment of dignity to every person by virtue of being human. Basic respect, he posits, is neither earned nor withdrawn; it is "non-reciprocal," "essentially inalienable," and prohibits the detestation, degradation, or dehumanization of all people.[3]

Even though respect honors human dignity, and is inalienably endowed to all persons, whether or not it is socially upheld is dictated by the social context in which people find themselves. By this I mean that since human beings are social beings, how an individual's human dignity is recognized/honored or not recognized/honored is defined by the dynamics of social power relations in which the individual is imbricated by virtue of, among other factors, her or his social positioning as well as her or his social roles, such as that of mothering.[4]

Mothers of Black sons in the United States find themselves situated at the intersection of two dominant social forces: patriarchal ideology of mothering and anti-Black racism. To elaborate, mothering entails nurturing, which includes affirming a child's personhood by upholding his or her human dignity (basic respect). Mothering also entails the socialization imperative: the socially imposed parental responsibility to transmit to the offspring the ideas, practices, attitudes, and values of the society in which they are being raised. This means, among other things, helping male children inculcate and conform to society's masculine gender norms. For mothers of Black sons, the socialization imperative is a tall order as the society into which they are to socialize their sons to become men, that is, to develop a masculine-gender identity, is imbued with anti-Black racism. As a result, the society is hostile to their sons' race and, through its race-based ideology and supporting social systems, structures, and institutions, calls into question the human dignity, the basic respect, of their sons. It should be of little surprise, then, that mothering at the juncture of such powerful social forces as are patriarchy and anti-Black racism in the United States is quite a predicament as it is fraught with complexity and contradictions and generates tremendous maternal angst, which may explain the fear, frustration, pain, and guilt that many of us mothers of Black sons experience.

The complexity and contradictions that plague mothering Black males begin with the institution of motherhood itself, a social conundrum for women, to say the least. Mothering has tremendous social capital in patriarchal cultures, for, as the initial and primary mode of socializing children, it is revered. Ann Crittenden reminds us that in the United States, there is no social institution more sacrosanct than motherhood, and no figure praised more fulsomely than that of the mother.[5] But, paradoxically, the act of mothering involves passing on to the children patriarchal ideas, attitudes, and values, in essence, the very patriarchal ideology by which mothers themselves, as female human beings, are subordinated and subjugated.

Added to this quandary, of being simultaneously valued for being a primary agent of patriarchal socialization and devalued for being female, mothers of Black sons in the United States have the additional weight of dealing with race-based subordination. As mothers, they are expected to prepare their children to live in a racially hostile society. These mothers are tortured by the unsettling knowledge that their sons are sites of public enunciations (social billboards, if you will) of anti-Black racism. They fear that their boys are targets or potential targets of unrelenting police profiling and heavy surveillance, and of social monitoring and public brutality. They are troubled that their sons belong to a social group that has a disproportionately high rate of incarceration but an abysmally low rate of education and employment.

The media's interest in and coverage of the recent violent deaths of Black men, such as Eric Garner, Michael Brown, John Crawford III, and Trayvon Martin, have brought public attention to the little regard the society, through its institutions, shows for the lives of Black men. Following these and other deadly assaults on Black men, much has been said, and rightly so, about the militarization of the police in the United States, the failure of the justice system to protect Black lives, and police brutality. Even the FBI director, James B. Comey, felt compelled to speak publicly about the rancor that often defines law enforcement's relationship with certain Black communities in America.[6] Also of serious concern to mothers of Black sons is Black-on-Black crime, to which, as Lisa Miller asserts, both the government and society assume a posture of powerlessness, sending the message that such crimes are incomprehensible and not much can be done about them.[7]

Though, unarguably, the most egregious, violence is but one of many major social threats to Black existence in the United States. The threats are pervasive and exist in all major social institutions. Mothers of Black sons are frustrated about race- and social class-based unequal funding of education that restricts working-class Blacks' access to quality education. These mothers are also anxious about the employment possibilities available to their sons, as work in American patriarchal culture is closely tied to a man's self-worth. These mothers fear that their sons' lack of, or restricted access to, gainful employment calls into question their sons' dignity and positive sense of self, which undermines these males' basic respect.

Many of the social impediments that Black males face have roots in U.S. society's historical and cultural conception of black masculinity as pathological and subhuman, particularly as endowed with excessive/hyper traits driven by emotion rather than reason and logic. Black males are conceived as hyper-aggressive, therefore excessively violent; hyper-sexual, therefore sexually threatening to (white) women; and, hyperactive, uncontrollably wild, undisciplined, therefore requiring medication to be managed in the classroom. Such constructions make it easy to ignore the humanity of Black males, to erase their personhood, and to fail or refuse to uphold their respect. Moreover, in such contexts, it is Black males' demand for basic respect that makes them the walking dead, beaten and bruised, strangled and suffocated, pierced with bullets, and left in public view (in streets, sidewalks, gutters, and more) for all to see their socially imposed race-based subhumanity.

But how can the mother of a Black son play a crucial role in offsetting the lack of respect from a society that fundamentally devalues and disrespects Black males? How does she at one and the same time affirm her son's personhood *and* socialize him to conform to the norms of the society, many of which place his dignity as a human being in jeopardy? This is a daunting task, indeed, one that generates internal conflict that is expressed in the often contradictory socializing messaging these mothers give to their sons. Researchers Howard, Rose, and Barbarin come to a similar conclusion in their study regarding how African American boys are socialized into racial and gender identities.[8] They found that mothers, similar to fathers, socialize their Black sons to acquire traditional patriarchally ascribed masculine values of individuality, autonomy, and competition, and simultaneously try to instill in their boys contrasting values in their racial socializing communications. It is noteworthy that the parents' racial socializing messages of communalism and cooperation are often viewed as feminine rather than masculine values in patriarchal cultures. As these researchers quite correctly surmise, the messaging conflict may be a consequence of trying to instill in the sons "traditional beliefs of being African American and being a man."[9]

Many mothers of Black sons can see no way out of this predicament if they wish to prepare their sons to live in the United States. I believe that this is the source of our maternal angst. How can we without pain tell our sons, as does Barbara Brandon-Croft, that they can "[r]each for the stars, but be prepared to be smacked down"? What degree of deference to or fear of law enforcement officers requires us to tell our Black males to be ultra-polite to police officers, fake officers included, as we would rather have our sons "humbled than harmed"?[10] What prepares us to handle the anger and frustration when teaching our sons about the unfairness of the society's race-based double standard that they will surely experience at work and play? [11] What calms our hearts in those constant yet fleeting moments of panic when it hits us that we are raising males to perform in the domain of dueling masculinities with their hands tied behind their backs?

The maternal angst is real, and, as I have attempted to show in this essay, it is rooted in the precarious position in which we, who mother Black sons, find ourselves. It is important for us to understand our predicament, but we should not allow ourselves to be arrested by our fears and anxieties or frustrations and guilt. We are not socially ill equipped to raise Black sons because we are mothers, as many would have us believe. To the contrary, we can use our voices as mothers to bring sustained attention to issues of social injustice, focusing in particular on specific issues that seriously affect the existence of our sons. These issues include the relationship between the high incarceration rate of Black men and the U.S. prison-industrial complex, quality education for working-class children, "Black-on-Black crime," the often unhealthy relationship between law enforcement and Black communities, among many others.

We must be pragmatic and be prepared to use the resources we have to challenge oppression wherever it exists, including that of our Black sons. As mothers in patriarchal cultures, we should recognize the social privilege of motherhood and the social capital that comes with it. Our society reveres motherhood and has empathy for a mother's agony.[12] Even though I am aware of the historical construction of Black motherhood in the United States and understand that reverence for motherhood may take us only so far, I wish to remain hopeful that empathy can go a long way, for example, in opening doors of congressional offices, getting time in the media, and encouraging Internet activism. As mothers, we must use the tools at hand in our struggle to ensure that our society recognizes and respects the humanity of our sons, our children, and of other groups that endure social detestation, degradation, or dehumanization.

16

A LONG WAYS FROM HOME?

Michele Moody-Adams

In 1956, the gospel singer Mahalia Jackson recorded a medley that combined two great American songs: George Gershwin's "Summertime" and the Negro Spiritual "Sometimes I Feel Like a Motherless Child."[1] Jackson's mellifluous performance seamlessly weaves the melodies together, showing just how fully the Gershwin song relies upon the tonal and rhythmic conventions of Black American music.[2] But her juxtaposition of the songs' lyrics is haunting and unsettling. The promise that "nothing can harm you," with daddy and mommy "standing by," offers a stark contrast to the sorrowful lament at sometimes feeling "a long ways from home," torn from the comfort of a loving mother and family. Yet Jackson understood that this contrast had long been at the core of what it is to be a Black mother in America, and perhaps especially at the center of what it is to be the mother of a Black son. The lyrics of "Summertime" express an ideal of motherhood that involves shielding one's young from the harsh realities of the world outside the family, but the words of the spiritual remind us that the realities of Black life in America have often thwarted Black women's efforts to realize that ideal. Now, well into the twenty-first century, the continued effects of anti-Black racism make the message that Mahalia Jackson delivered sixty years ago as timely as ever.

Of course, the mechanisms through which racism thwarts Black women's efforts to protect their sons have changed over time. The evils of chattel slavery were replaced by the indignities of lynching and post-Reconstruction Jim Crow laws; the anti–civil rights violence of the

1950s and 1960s gave way to "new Jim Crow" policies of mass incarceration in the 1980s and beyond.[3] But, in many respects, the challenges of mothering Black sons have remained the same. Black mothers still fear that, whatever they do, their sons will be treated as dangerous outsiders who must struggle to feel—and to be—"at home" in America. The continued reasonableness of that fear is confirmed by the recent spate of police and vigilante killings of unarmed Black males (sometimes as young as twelve).[4] Moreover, while it is clear that the racially disparate character of economic inequality intensifies the effects of anti-Black racism for many families, even the sons of the Black professional classes will sometimes confront the dangerous consequences of the reality that far too many white Americans believe that Black American males do not qualify as full citizens.

Mothers of Black sons usually feel the effects of such attitudes as soon as their children are old enough to be genuinely aware of the world outside the family. Thus, while the cultural ideal of what is required to be a good mother to a very young child requires one to erect a temporary boundary between the "personal" and the "political," that boundary has very little relevance to the real demands of mothering a Black son. Indeed, ironically, any mother of a Black son who tries too hard to separate the personal and the political runs the risk of being a spectacularly bad mother. This is because she can prepare her son to understand what it really means to be seen as a permanent possibility of danger only if she is ready to discuss the political realities of anti-Black racism fairly early in the child's life.[5] For instance, even a very young boy must understand that he may be subject to draconian and racially discriminatory disciplinary policies in elementary and middle school. Further, as he grows older, he must expect to be greeted with suspicion and mistrust in the most ordinary encounters in stores and simply walking down the street, and once he learns to drive, he will all too often be a target for harassment when he is behind the wheel of a car. He must, therefore, learn that if he reacts in the "wrong" way—which is often defined by a standard that assumes he is dangerous, whatever he does—the outcome of any encounter can be deadly. Of course, Black mothers of little girls must make many complicated decisions about how the realities of racial stereotyping and bias should shape their parenting. But as destructive and dangerous as the cultural constructions of Black femininity can be, they are rarely directly linked with the threat of incarceration or violent death as the cultural constructions of Black masculinity too often are.

These distorted constructions of Black masculinity make it difficult, if not virtually impossible, for young Black males to ever *really be* seen as children. Moreover, this artificial shortening of childhood can be especially devastating for the most socioeconomically disadvantaged families if a son ends up getting into some trouble with the law. Even if that "trouble" involves petty crime, it will often be presumed that in order to send a message that criminal behavior cannot be socially tolerated, the conduct must be dealt with harshly (and often more harshly than if the offenders were white). During the 1980s and 1990s, many Black Americans came to accept this presumption unquestioningly—often in desperation at the sense that there was no other way to address the rise of crime in urban neighborhoods. But, over time, the consequence of this presumption was that Black adolescence, especially for Black males in the least well-off American families, was effectively criminalized.

American society has remained essentially forgiving—and often remarkably lenient—toward some of the more serious "mistakes" made by young white adolescents, particularly when those mistakes involve the possession of drugs, and especially if the young people who make them are headed for college and, later, toward "respectable" careers. But under current practices, young Black males who commit petty crimes often end up just a step away from a life of incarceration. The problem is that once a petty offense draws a young person into the justice system, it gets more and more difficult for him to get out of that system. Time-consuming legal processes, and "doing time" in juvenile detention centers, will clearly disrupt a young person's schooling. Further, even if that young person finishes high school, employers and college admissions officers will often view him as a risky prospect. Most problematic of all, it is sometimes claimed that evidence of involvement in petty crimes, or sometimes just the suspicion of such involvement, can constitute partial "justification" for police brutality, or even for police and vigilante killings of unarmed Black males. Of course, lawlessness must be punished. But most reasonable people will acknowledge that death is hardly an appropriate punishment for petty theft. One must, then, wonder why it is ever thought defensible to reject that reasonable stance when the petty thief happens to be Black. In many urban neighborhoods, this cultural double standard is not only a means of defining a Black son's childhood out of existence, but of rendering him a "deserving" subject of institutional disregard.

The effort to help her child respond to this cultural double standard will present the concerned Black mother with yet another extraordinary set of challenges. One of the most critical challenges is figuring out how to help one's child navigate the best path between several different and competing visions of masculinity. First, a critical source of difficulty is the fact that the culturally dominant conception of masculinity is generally reserved for white males, even as it is continually held up as a standard against which to judge alleged failures of Black men to be "responsible." But second, the growing child must then contend with the thoroughly tainted conception of Black masculinity that is used to restrict access to important social goods, and sometimes to punish Black males as intrinsically dangerous "outsiders." In the last few decades, a third, and far more complex, conception of masculinity has emerged along with the cultures of urban rap and hip-hop. The challenges of deciding how to respond to this new development are considerable.

To be sure, the politically insightful music of many early rappers had a cultural potential that, in some respects, was not unlike that of the Negro Spirituals in their day: it often expressed both the struggles and the genuine political hopes of the generation that produced it. But, in contrast to the political subtlety of early rap music, all too often, contemporary hip-hop music offers images of Black masculinity that are less constructive. They are either too bound up with a purely oppositional "outlaw" stance to be politically empowering, or they are too mired in the crass materialism and the dangerous misogyny of the dominant culture to be a source of constructive political and economic change. Regrettably, it is the latter aspect of contemporary hip hop— the celebration of materialism and misogyny—that has made its way into the American mainstream, and that is all too easily translated back into the destructive idiom of mainstream racism. When this happens, there is a risk that hip-hop culture will not only strengthen cultural biases against Black men but that it will also reaffirm destructive cultural biases against Black women.[6]

But perhaps the most problematic development in this domain is that far too many Americans who are not Black are simply willing to discount the validity of a fourth conception of Black masculinity—that conception that is embodied in the lives of all the hard-working, Black American men who have consistently "played by the rules" of American society. Regrettably, those critics of President Obama who have consistently sought to prove that he is not really American are evidence of just how powerful this effort to discount constructive models of Black American masculinity can be. The persistence of the anti-Obama "birther" movement suggests that one of the most important challenges for African Americans generally—and not just for mothers of Black sons— is to find some means to increase cultural acceptance and appreciation of all the varied and constructive models of Black masculinity there are. We need to find a way to tell the stories of those Black men—like my own father, among so many others—who not only succeeded in spite of the destructive effects of racism, but who continued to believe that an America that lived up to its stated ideals might eventually make it possible for more Black men to find their own path to a rewarding life.

Meeting that challenge is a daunting prospect. In the meantime, what else can the mother of a Black son do? How might she be an effective participant in efforts to change American culture and political institutions so that her children are no longer, in James Baldwin's words, "at the mercy of the reflexes the color of one's skin cause . . . in other people"?[7] I contend that exercising the power of the ballot may provide the most effective response. For instance, it is important to identify and support political leaders whom we can trust to repeal the legal provisions that—for too many families—have artificially shortened the length of Black childhood, criminalized Black adolescence, and treated American prisons as though they could be a substitute for job training and education. It is also important to support political leaders and public figures who insist that the persistence of economic inequality, along with the disappearance of work, endangers the futures of every American. There are far too many communities in America in which prisons are the main economic engine, providing the only reasonable employment for the rural and exurban populations who are hired to oversee the incarceration of the Black and brown men who have come to be overrepresented in prisons.

Finally, African Americans, generally, must try to create more constructive alternatives to the cultural alienation and disenfranchisement of Black males. For much of the twentieth century, African American political culture was dominated by lively "internal" disagreements about what those alternatives should look like. Should they be integrationist or separatist, religious or secular, committed to preserving racial identities or seeking to create a "post-racial" society? At the start of the twenty-first century, the question of whether to promote local versus global commitments must be added to the debate. But whatever the terms of the debate, the only real hope for addressing the alienation and disenfranchisement of Black males in America is to enlist Black men and Black women—and anyone concerned about racial justice—in the reinvigoration of the kind of Black political commitment that once made such debates so important and sometimes remarkably effective. If such efforts are to have lasting effects, that commitment must be strong and deep enough to last longer than any one presidential campaign and (as we learned from the recent struggles in Ferguson, Missouri) it must take local and municipal elections to be as momentous in shaping daily life (if not more so) as any national elections.

Renewed political commitment must also be accompanied by support for a cultural renaissance that might allow for a fuller expression of the complexity of Black American life. That complexity must be more fully represented in literature, history, movies, and television to better document the ways in which the accomplishments and the sacrifices of countless Black men and women have helped to bring America closer to realizing its most cherished ideals. To be sure, their sacrifices have not yet managed to make this country a fully welcoming home for Black Americans. But for the sake of all of our children, we have a duty to respect and celebrate the courage and devotion of those men and women who never let despair overwhelm political hope.

17

T.H.U.G. (TALENTED, HUMANISTIC, UNIQUE, GIFTED)

Anthropology, Sentiments, and Narratives of Black
Mothers and Sons

Elisha Oliver

AN INTRODUCTION IN THE KEY OF ACADEMY

As academics, we strive to explore and explain the ways in which
individuals and groups function and exist. We examine behaviors, experiences, emotions, actions, and reactions.[1] We use our authoritative lens
and frameworks to "make sense" of the scripts we are seeing, hearing,
and often, ourselves, deeply and personally experiencing. Exploration
and examination of the life-ways and experiences of individuals and
groups not only shed light on the ways in which others are organized
and function but enable theoreticians, anthropologists, and other researchers to explore and observe their own experiences with a reflexive
lens. We are able to participate in the experience and performance of
the human condition of those whom we study while also reflecting on
our own attached sentiments to such experiences and observations.

Anthropology, like many other disciplines, speaks volumes about the
human condition. Anthropology involves observations of humankind at
its worst and best and also serves as an apparatus to explore relationships and tensions that exist within social systems. These relationships
and tensions are underpinned with scripts of sentiments. Raymond
Williams posits that "social forms are evidently more recognizable when

they are articulate and explicit."[2] This is applicable to sentiments that we internally and externally participate in and observe.

Sentiments can be understood through a variety of explorations. The ways in which individuals and collectives conceptualize, internalize, and (re)act upon sentiments are diverse. The experiences of sentiments are both individual and collective. These experiences are implicit and explicit, and they bind and dismantle categories of being. Reflecting on Michel Foucault's concept of (his)tory, we note that the life-ways, patterns, and social conditions are never exactly the same or as they seem. According to Foucault "history is the concrete body of a development, with its moments of intensity, its lapses, its extended periods of feverish agitation, its fainting spells."[3] He goes on to posit that "genealogy does not pretend to go back in time to restore an unbroken continuity that operates beyond the dispersion of forgotten things; its duty is not to demonstrate that the past actively exists in the present, that it continues secretly to animate the present having imposed a predetermined form on all its vicissitudes."[4] For the reading of the narrative and missive contained here, it is important to (re)member Foucault's suppositions, especially as Black Motherhood, sons, and reflexivity are explored within intimate ethnographic case studies that are both experimental and autobiographical on the part of the writer who has decided to share her story.

The relationship between the histories and memories of the individuals in this chapter is neither horizontal nor vertical. There is no single directionality. The histories associated with memories often shift, slip, and are inverted to make sense of what has happened in the past and what is happening in the present. The questions here are: how are sentiments inscribed onto a racial history of motherhood and fear; how is history inscribed onto sentiments; and, how do such questions map memories of the preconscious, conscious, and unconscious when examining the production, distribution, and consumption of race-related histories, current events, fears, and memories? I neither portend nor offer an answer or conclusion to these questions. I leave the reader to draw his or her own conclusion(s), to critically interrogate the past and the present as both relate to the treatment of Black sons, to construct his or her own questions, and to enter openly and honestly into a constructive dialogue that fosters and facilitates change. I offer a chimera of sorts, a narrative that encompasses the narrative teller, the writer, and you, the reader. I offer a space, a digital page, a fragment of a recycled washed, rewashed, and bleached tree, a paper, a script in which a narrative and a missive is produced, distributed, and consumed. I am between Scylla and Charybdis. I can't tell the narrative of another without telling my own.

"But the color of a Negro's skin makes him easily recognizable, makes him suspect, converts him into a defenseless target."
—Richard Wright, *Black Boy*, 1944

TALENTED AND UNIQUE: THE NARRATIVE OF *PREVIOUS*

I watched the little boy struggle with the bags of groceries from my porch across the street. It was early morning; yet, the temperature was beginning to climb well into the nineties. He was wearing no shirt, nor shoes and the apparatus that once served as a connector port for feeding tubes caught the summer sun and glimmered like a shiny coin against his frail umber body. His mother and two sisters trailed behind him. A group of men were standing at the corner drinking beer as the small family passed. They made no attempts to offer any assistance to the little boy struggling and weighted down with the bags of groceries. I continued to watch as this little group made their way home. As they finally reached their door, I reflected on the story his mother had shared with me one evening when she came to question me about the bag of snacks I had given him.

"They shot my brother first," she said, beginning to share a story that would provide some explanation regarding her own traumatic life history, the physical and mental ailments that afflicted her three living children, and the feeling of fear that rears its ugly head when her son is not in her presence. *"I was pregnant with my daughter, 'Suddenly,' and needed a fix. I didn't have no money but was willing to do some things, you know,"* she went on. *"My brother and I went down to this white guy's house. He had a reputation for being a mean ass biker but he was the guy to go to when you needed something and couldn't pay with cash. Just as I was about to go back into the room with Red, they [the police] kicked down the door. Guns were drawn, there was screaming but the only sound that I really remember is the sound of the gun that shot my brother. One of the cops shot him. They thought he had a gun. I*

had a bad feeling about going to Red's place that day but I really needed a hit. I couldn't help it then, and now, some days I still can't help it. I don't do the hard stuff no more, just a drink and smoke here and there to help with the stress and fear. Ain't nobody tryin' to help me make sure my son has a better life than me and some nights I'm so afraid that he ain't gonna make it."

*"Sometimes, I can't get out the bed unless I have me a drink and a smoke because the fear of something happening to my little boy by a cop that only sees a thug and not a smart, **talented,** and **unique** kid is chasing me like the devil chasing a sinner."* She was pristine in appearance; however, she reeked of liquor and cigarettes when we had this conversation. Her sad and empty eyes revealed signs of many sleepless nights that were filled with fear. Brenda, like many other women in this neighborhood feared the streets, feared the police, and feared the deep-seated racism that existed in the town. Her pristine appearance was only a mask for her seemingly disheveled life that was filled with fear and angst. I let her continue her story as she shared the many ways in which the little boy that struggled with the groceries had become the very talented and unique caregiver for his mother and sisters.

"Previous was born with so many health issues, you know. He's a little genius, just so smart and talented," she went on to share. I continued to sit and listen as Brenda gushed with pride, like any mother would do when she speaks of her child. *"It was touch and go with him and his health for a while,"* she explained. *"I was so afraid he wasn't gonna make it. It's sad but I'm still afraid that he ain't gonna make it; not because of his health but because of the history of this town. It's just so prejudiced here. People are racist. The cops look at me for what I used to be. They judge my kids, especially my boy, by what I used to be, by what my brother used to be. They don't realize that my little boy is the reason why I'm doing better today, why I'm enrolled at the vo-tech, why I have a little job at the Walmart, and why my girls are doing better. All they see is a little Black Boy from the poor area of town and they automatically assume he's a thief, a future thug. He ain't though! He cooks, cleans, helps me with the girls, and tells me, Momma, it's gone be okay while holding my hand when all seems hopeless. He's unique like that . . . always looking on the bright side when the world we live in ain't always bright for us. I want them [those that hate and fear Previous because the color of his skin] to see his talent, his unique ability to*

love when others don't love him." As Brenda continued to talk about her son and explain her fears, I began to think about my own son, David. Brenda spent hours discussing Emmett Till, Michael Brown, her brother, and countless others that were victims of a Black American genocide. I would spend several more hours reconciling my own feelings of joy in motherhood with fear in motherhood.

HUMANISTIC AND GIFTED: A MISSIVE FOR DAVID

"I grew up in the South under segregation. So, I know what terrorism feels like—when your father could be taken out in the middle of the night and lynched just because he didn't look like he was in an obeying frame of mind when a white person said something he must do. I mean, that's terrorism, too."
—Alice Walker[5]

"I am always interested in the representations of strength in women, where that strength comes from, how it is called upon when it is needed most, and what it costs for a woman to be strong."
—Roxane Gay[6]

Dear David,

Hey Son, momma has been doing what momma does, being an anthropologist. I've been collecting narratives from other mothers that look like me. We share the same hopes and dreams and sadly, the same fears for our sons. We, along with other mothers of color across the United States, are members of an imagined community, a very unique sorority. We have mothered Black Sons, talented, humanistic, unique, and gifted sons. Motherhood has bound us inextricably to one another.

David, as I recount the narratives that have been shared with me, I am faced with my own fears. You were born into this world with a heart full of compassion and love for everyone. You have always been **humanistic***. Your every action is performed with an unparalleled kindness. When we spoke last week, you mentioned training for your second marathon. The excitement in your voice was cute and innocent. It reminded me of you at six as you described all that you had learned about Egyptian mummies; however, as your excitement filled the phone as you explained your training schedule, my fear grew. I immediately began to think of training alternatives because I didn't (don't) want you running* through your neighborhood in a hoodie. I didn't (don't) want someone (the police) to see you, a gentle giant, my son, as a threatening 6'5 Black Man that, surely, "must be up to no good."

David, they won't know that you're **gifted.** They won't know that you're working towards an MBA, that you play the violin and the guitar, and that you pray every night for those you love and those that don't love you. They won't know that you love your family which includes a cat and a dog that you adopted to save from euthanasia. They will only see what their ignorance and fear allows them to see, a "big black threatening man."

I sometimes feel as if Black Mothers are experiencing home-grown terrorism. Where is the protection for our sons? Where is your protection? I feel an urgency to train for the marathon, too, bad knees and all, just so I can make certain you're safe. I know Son, I can hear you in my mind, it (me training alongside you) is a crazy idea. I recognize and acknowledge this; however, I also recognize and acknowledge that the world in which we live is no longer a safe place for a mother's most precious gift, her child.

David, I look at motherhood from the past to the present, from slavery to this very moment and I wonder where the wellspring of strength comes from for the mothers that have lost a son because of ignorant ideologies. I am strong, Son, but momma can't bear the thought of losing you. My world would be undone . . . , and then there would just be hell to pay, 'cause momma don't play that! I digress; I am caught up in anger and emotion.

I do want you to be aware of the day in which we live. Things are not as they appear. Certain racisms and prejudices lurk about like monsters in the dark. Our society is (re)experiencing a moral and ethical delay and until change occurs, be aware. Be safe and know that you are loved.

—Momma

OUR SONS: LIFE AND LIBERTY

In reviewing the foundation for historical thought and philosophical discourse as it relates to the whole of humanity, certain ideologies, arguments, and discourses are disjointed. Based on the definition(s) of liberalism, history does not always illustrate a nonviolent social philosophy that advocates freedom, development in all spheres of human endeavor, and governmental guarantees of individual rights and civil liberties regardless of the person. Norbert Elias writes, "This basic tissue resulting from many single plans and actions of men can give rise to changes and patterns that no individual person has planned or created. From this interdependence of people arises an order sui generis, an order more compelling and stronger than the will and reason of the individual people composing it."[7] Our sons are not thugs whose lives bear no value. Ours are Talented, Humanistic, Unique, and Gifted Sons that are in a class of their own. They should be valued and afforded the same civil liberties as others that differ phenotypically. The time to stand against inequality is now. The time to protect our sons (and daughters) is now.

18

A FIERCE LOVE

The Unique Process of Nurturing, Educating, and
Protecting Our Black Sons

Tracey McCants Lewis

THE COMING OF THE STRONG BLACK MAN

Recent population projections predict that by the year 2044, the United States will be a "minority majority" nation, with approximately 12.7 percent of the total 50.3 percent minority population being Black.[1] The truth of the matter is that a number of people in this world are not prepared to face a strong, confident, educated Black man, even in the year 2016.[2] Years ago, I experienced many disconcerting examples of how a Black male's strong sense of self could be feared, misunderstood, and resented. I only truly recognized this unsettling pattern of thinking when I became a mother of a Black male child. When my son was accepted into a pre-kindergarten program, my ex-husband and I were assured by the admissions counselor that it was a very diverse class. However, on the first day of school, we learned that he was the only student of color enrolled in the class. We decided to keep him in the school, but soon realized that the aversion to Black male confidence is a destructive pattern of thinking exposed even in pre-kindergarten.

MISPERCEPTIONS OF BLACK INNOCENCE

My ex-husband and I began receiving daily calls, notes, and e-mails from our son's teachers about something he had done that day that was of concern. One of the first trivial issues presented to us was a concern that we did not supply a *"lovey"*[3] for him to use at school. My initial question for his teachers was, "What is a *lovey*?" I was curtly informed that a *lovey* was a blanket or a stuffed animal that a child should bring to school to aid in his or her transition to nap time. I responded that my son never needed a *lovey* to fall asleep.[4] I further inquired if he was having difficulty transitioning to nap time at school and was told that he was not. His teachers were concerned that the absence and lack of need for a lovey was synonymous with aggression. My ex-husband and I recognized this *concern* was an attempt to label our four-year-old son based upon their preconceived notions of Blackness because his teachers could not understand why he did not need, but the rest of his classmates, all white, did need, a lovey.[5]

The second example of many involved a call from these same teachers about his physical stamina and ability. We were informed that they were again *concerned* that our son was too aggressive and did not have the capacity to appreciate risks. This call stemmed from a day on the playground and my son's use of some playground equipment. We were told that when the children were taken outside for recess that my son began playing on the jungle gym with other children, but unlike his classmates, he was going back and forth doing a hand-over-hand technique on the horizontal ladder. The teachers admitted that he was doing it properly and did not get injured, but scorned that he should not have the ability to do that yet at his age. They further chided that he should have been afraid to play on this equipment, but that his aggressive nature and failure to appreciate risks clouded his four-year-old judgment.

These two brief stories illustrate how some young Black males are viewed and labeled at a young age—almost from birth. My position as the mother of a Black male child has been to love him unconditionally, nurture him, correct him, and educate him. These duties are no different from any mother's of any other race or ethnicity, but there are some marked and unique distinctions dictated by the circumstances of our society.[6] Like any mother, I think about my child every day and pray for him. My daily prayer is something like this, "Lord, please bless my child today. Please put a hedge of protection around him and keep him from all hurt, harm, and danger. In Jesus' name I pray. Amen." I know this prayer is similar to the prayers of all mothers for their children. My prayer is not only for my son's general safety and well-being, but also to protect him from any harm that may be directed at him because of the color of his skin. There are some in our world who would believe that my son is dangerous or aggressive, not based upon the tone of his voice, his stature, or an articulated threat, but merely based upon the color of his skin, brown, and his gender, male. My son and I share a deep mahogany skin tone that is threatening to some and to others a form of intrigue.[7]

ABANDONMENT OF *INNOCENT UNTIL PROVEN GUILTY*

Many young Black men are stopped and questioned by police because they *"fit a description"* of a suspect, someone of interest, or someone suspicious. *Black's Law Dictionary* defines suspicious as "the act of suspecting, or the state of being suspected; imagination, generally of something ill; distrust; mistrust; doubt. Suspicion implies a belief or opinion based upon facts or circumstances which do not amount to proof." [8] An oft-repeated theme of some encounters of Black males with police officers is that there is a presumption of immediate guilt.

The summer and fall of 2014 featured national headlines of stories detailing the deaths of Black males (including a twelve-year-old child) who were unarmed. Some of these incidents were captured on video, thereby allowing the world to observe for itself what some believe to be extreme instances of perceived guilt.[9]

Eric Garner (Age 43)—killed July 17, 2014, Staten Island, New York, by a New York Police Department officer during an illegal choke-hold. A video was recorded depicting the altercation between Mr. Garner and the police officers, including the fatal chokehold and Mr. Garner's last words repeated a haunting eleven times, "I can't breathe."[10] Mr. Garner was being arrested for the sale of untaxed cigarettes.[11] **John Crawford (Age 22)**—killed August 5, 2014, Beavercreek, Ohio, by a Beavercreek police officer called to a local Wal-Mart after receiving a 9-1-1 call about a Black male waving a gun at customers in the store.[12] He was shot twice by an officer, and the gun was determined to be a BB gun sold in the Wal-Mart store. **Michael Brown (Age 18)**—killed August 9, 2014, Ferguson, Missouri, by a Ferguson police officer after he was ordered to move out of the street to the sidewalk. Eyewitnesses alleged that Michael Brown was shot by the officer while his hands were up in the air in a form of surrender. **Ezell Ford Jr. (Age 25)**— killed August 11, 2014, Los Angeles, by an L.A. police officer during an alleged altercation with two police officers. A witness account indicated that Mr. Ford was complying with the officers' commands when he was shot. **Tamir Rice (Age 12)**—killed November 22, 2014, Cleveland, Ohio, by a Cleveland police officer who responded with his partner to a 9-1-1 call about a young man walking around with a gun, pointing it at people. The 9-1-1 caller noted that the gun was "probably a fake," but he was scared.[13] Surveillance video of the incident shows a police car racing to the scene, just feet away from Tamir Rice, and an officer immediately opening fire upon the twelve-year-old child. It does not appear from the video that Tamir was given an opportunity to comply with any directive from the officer before being shot twice.[14]

These men and child were not able to experience the presumption of innocence[15] afforded to them in a court of law because they were killed. These men and child were not given the benefit, like their white counterparts, to *Crime While White*.[16] Numerous hypotheses can be rendered after observing the videos of the incidents noted above. One common theory that intertwines their deaths is that these human beings of various hues of brown were immediately perceived as a threat, per-ceived as dangerous, perceived as aggressive, perceived to be subhu-man.[17] They were not given the benefit of the presumption of inno-cence. Split-second decisions to discharge a weapon or invoke a choke-hold led to their deaths. Another disturbing factor seen in over half of the videos and reports afterward is the negligent failure to render im-mediate medical attention for their injuries or to secure the crime scene in a humane and appropriate manner.[18] One can assume from the videos and comments of the officers that their perceptions, biases, fears, and preconceived notions resulted in these tragic deaths.

LOVE

I recently attended the 4th Annual Adonai Young Men's Conference[19] and had the opportunity to ask some Black teenage boys what they most desire from their mothers. The overwhelming response received was . . . love. These young men want to know that we love them and that we are there for them always; that we carry a fierce love for them that nurtures, educates, prepares, and protects them. The fierce love that I have for my son has imbued him with positive self-images to counter the irrational biases, fears, and misconceptions that some people allow to daunt their being.

Black mothers (and mothers of Black sons), I implore you, we must continually build up our sons from infants to adults. We must nurture them with understanding, care, and love to deconstruct any building blocks of labels, misconceptions, misunderstandings, or hatred that they encounter at school, work, or in their surroundings. We must be cognizant to greet any young Black man that we see with a warm greeting, which reminds them that they are loved fiercely.

"Darkness cannot drive out darkness: only light can do that. Hate cannot drive out hate: only love can do that."

—Dr. Martin Luther King Jr.

19

THROUGH THE VALLEY OF THE SHADOW OF DEATH

Veronica T. Watson

Yea, though I walk through the valley of the shadow of death, I will fear no evil: for thou art with me; thy rod and thy staff they comfort me.—Psalm 23

I am both a lover and a teacher of African American literature. I am a researcher whose work on whiteness is grounded in the African American experience, the insights into and analyses of whiteness that Black writers have made from the beginning of that literary tradition in the United States. I am a person who has examined white violence as part of my scholarly efforts, but also as part of my human efforts. I have scratched at it as one picks at an itchy scar left over from a more serious wound. I have hoped that the itchiness was a sign of healing—my incessant need to return to that site of trauma a commitment never to forget. But in my soul, I have known that it was more than that. As I scoured the books, poems, sermons, and songs of our history, I have been looking for the thing that helped Black mothers to carry on in the face of so much pain, fear, and uncertainty. Because I haven't always known how to carry on. I haven't always been sure of how to raise my son to be a Black man in a nation that despises his existence, a country that would more easily end his life than it would make an effort to save it.

I've been seeking the book of tips and tricks and prayers that Black mothers surely created in their sojourn: what to say about the world our sons were entering, what not to say; what to scold about that might save their lives, when to urge them to fight. What to teach them about defiance and righteous outrage and how to operate in a system where their actions, however small, might cause their very lives to be snatched. How to impress upon them that they are not the sum total of the images of Black men that saturate our screens, making their dreams and talents seem trivial, or even worse, futile. How to mourn with them and send them back out when they come to know how imperiled they are. How to prepare *my* beautiful brown boy to be a strong, loving, compassionate, God-fearing Black man able to make a difference in a world that needs so much to be changed . . . well, there's no instruction manual for that.

The list of names is long—decades long, centuries long. Black men cut down for standing up. Black men assassinated for speaking, terminated for looking, butchered for breathing. Another African American man-child is shot dead. Twelve years old. How many is that? Tamir Rice's crime on November 22, 2014? Playing on a Cleveland playground with a play gun that looked too real. Within twenty seconds of the police arriving on the scene, our son was dead. His sister—who could have been a mother, aunt, or friend, it would have made no difference—prevented from comforting him. Instead, her love and compassion were shut up in a police cruiser; she forced to witness the horror unfolding before her, equally alone.

Where has the compassion and humanity of those officers been shut up? What was shut off in them that they could not see our son, a child, probably playing cops and robbers where he imagined himself as the man behind the shield, serving and protecting? I cannot help but to look over at my son, also twelve, an imaginative child who dives into shadows to "ninja" his sister and dreams up new starship designs with his Legos. I sense in his hesitant questions, his flipping of the television from the news reports of Black men dead, that he is aware of how precarious his life is as a young Black man in this country. But I don't know which is better, to pray for him to understand or to pray that he never knows: that some random white man or woman, in some random place, might one day decide, without forethought or afterthought, that their white bodies are in imminent danger just by being in proximity to his. Their whiteness always already constructed as endangered and under siege while my brown sons are always already, the menace that legitimates and justifies their fear. Will knowledge or ignorance of the continuing realities of racism make it easier for him to feel that his life matters?

George Yancy talks about this practice of social inscription as the act of "confiscating" Black bodies; Michelle Alexander and others demonstrate the material effects of racial scripting of Black male bodies: the surveillance, harassment, criminalization, mass incarceration, and death of Black and brown bodies. Although "death" is perhaps too passive, too neutral. "Death" is something that happens to all people, is part of our humanity. What our sons are experiencing is more active, directed at their bodies and spirits, and more sinister for the myriad ways it is made to seem inevitable, even reasonable. According to Representative Elijah Cummings in a "Face the Nation" interview broadcast on January 4, 2015, "96% of 400 or so deaths by police officers were white officers killing African Americans."[1] Three hundred eighty-four Black lives and many still argue there is no epidemic, no problem. How do I explain to my son that he may one day be pulled over by a police officer for no reason he can discern (driving while Black)? That he may be followed through a department store he enters to shop for a new pair of jeans (shopping while Black)? Or asked nicely, or menacingly, "What are you doing here?" while visiting a friend across town (*being* while Black)? And how do we explain that any of these moments could escalate into an even greater tragedy if he is not careful, while concealing our deepest fear that even if he *is* careful . . .

A howling chasm opens in my soul as I wonder what in the world I can do to protect him, protect them, from the madness of racism that so very few will even acknowledge exists. It's a question that links me to three hundred years of history and innumerable ancestors on these shores.

As a critical-whiteness scholar who is also an African Americanist, the recent rash of murders at the hands of white law enforcement officers engages a particular type of reflection for me. It calls up a particular history. Other families and communities denied access to loved ones, forced to be voiceless witnesses. Warned, in that imposed silence, of our own vulnerability. What is all of the noise about body cameras turning things around, as if seeing is all that is needed? We have the footage and still refuse to see, to hear. No billed, yet again. Acquitted, yet again. Our sons, our voices, our experiences, our *lives*, are disbelieved, disregarded, discounted, and dismembered. I CAN'T BREATHE.

Where do I turn to make sense of this new era of white terror, this backlash against Black mobility and achievement even though so many of us do not feel like we have, or can move much at all? In her work on trauma, activist Laura Van Dernoot Lipsky argues that one of the symptoms that manifests among people who are caretakers to those who have been traumatized is hypervigilance, "a dynamic of being wholly focused on our job, to the extent that being present for anything else in our life can seem impossible."[2] As I have written elsewhere with Becky Thompson,

> What an apt description of whiteness. When considered from the vantage point of racial trauma, whiteness can certainly be understood as having been "wholly focused on [the] job" of defining, policing and protecting white privilege, space, identity, and culture. Collectively, it has drawn boundaries, defined an inside and an outside to a presumed-sacred space/identity, and aggressively ejected and rejected those bodies that fall outside of the ideological and social pale.[3]

When racial hypervigilance casts people of color as criminal outsiders to a nation, death follows. We've seen it throughout the twentieth century around the globe: South Africa, Germany, the Balkans, the UK, the United States. When the machinery of a nation—everything from politics to religion and science to entertainment—is made to support one argument, one view, one vision of a nation's identity, those who do not fit that imagined script are made disposable. Physically, emotionally, psychologically, intellectually, we are disposed of. Our bodies fall. Outside. Are left lying on streets, on cold park grounds, swinging in trees, bubbling down in murky creeks. The only thing rising is our scream.

I am fortunate to have a husband, a life partner, who is a pragmatist. He writhes and struggles and cries out ("I have to teach my son things as a black man that no white father ever has to teach his white son!"), but he has those conversations nonetheless. "If you're stopped by the police, be respectful. Keep your hands visible. Announce what you're doing *before* you move." But our son is too young, I used to think, to teach him *those* skills. That was before. Now I must reckon with my truth. I haven't brought myself to those conversations, not because he is young but because something in me refuses. I don't want to teach my son to bow to the insanity of a hypervigilant whiteness or policing that is criminal. I don't want to find a way to make crazy seem sane, to stammer and stutter my way through a lesson that makes this seem normal. Though it is ordinary for far too many of us.

Instead, I choose to teach him/us the history of our people, those who conquered their own fear and the terror that was imposed on them and changed an unjust world. My words will remind him of what he already is coming to know, that the work is not yet finished because the system still values some lives more than others, still protects some persons while sacrificing others, and still blames those it has eviscerated for having bowels, lungs, and heart. My lessons, which I hope will complement those his father shares, will be different now that I'm talking, because tragically, twelve is not too young to prepare him for the threats that face Black men every day. We don't have the luxury of childhood. Perhaps this is the beginning of that instruction manual I have been longing to find:

> Son, don't resist arrest or questioning. Make eye contact. Speak up. If you sense the police about to take action that involves you, make your way to a public space where others can witness for you if you can. Pay attention to the time, your surroundings. Get a badge number. Get a name. If you can't get to a crowd, make that technology that you know so well, that is always so present, work for you. Call a friend and leave the line open. Hit record on your device. That action may provide proof that you were not belligerent or angry. If you see that you're about to have an encounter, snap a selfie. It may become a visual record that your face was not battered by a previous altercation. If things are violently escalating despite your efforts, call out to a stranger to call 9-1-1. Say it multiple times. Say it loudly. If the encounter is being taped by someone, as so many are these days, you want your voice to be heard too. Never refuse the search, field test, or question, but defer, "I have no problem with that, officer, and will happily comply as soon as my attorney arrives." Be cooperative, but exercise your rights. Be smart. Survive. And then, if you are in the right, fight back.

20

MOTHERS AND THEIR BLACK SONS
Struggling against Fears, Sorrows, and Hope

Blanche Radford-Curry

Too often the mothers of Black sons are tired of being tired in their struggle against their fears, sorrows, and hope for the future of their sons. They hope that their Black sons' future is brighter than theirs. It is a hope for real freedom, equality, dignity, justice, opportunity, and success far greater than theirs. Why not the same hope for her Black sons as the hope of other mothers for their sons? Their hope for their Black sons is "a dream deferred"[1] for them. While they are willing to defer this dream for themselves, too often neither their sacrifices nor their hopes for their Black sons are enough. They know of the racism so engrained in the fabric of America that continues to defer this dream. Their struggle against encounters of racist acts upon their Black sons has been long lived, beginning from infancy. Moreover, they have lived with the reality of racism being constantly demonstrated in various ways by whites in the life journey of their Black sons. The pain of their Black sons' lives viewed as "less than," devalued as human beings, and treated without respect is real for them.

While tired of their struggles against racist encounters of their Black sons, these mothers manage to sustain this struggle for the sake of the hope they have for their Black sons. They know and understand, first, that the history of racism in American history existed long before they were born and, second, the W. E. B. DuBois phrase that the problem of the twentieth century will be racism and its continuation and overwhelming impact on their Black sons into the twenty-first century. Their struggles against racism echo and ring déjà vu some of my own experience years ago. I, along with other mothers, shared our personal stories of racism experienced by our children from different perspectives. We shared our struggles against this racism so deeply woven throughout the fabric of North American history.

In my essay "Mothers Confronting Racism: Transforming the Lives of Our Children and Others,"[2] I spoke of the racism experienced by both my young daughter and son. As I spoke about my attempt to repair the sting of racism to my son's self-esteem, I learned of other neighboring mothers' stories of their Black sons. They shared stories about their Black teenage sons being stopped frequently by police officers to the extent that their self-esteem had been stifled and about how these Black sons were reluctant to drive to school, work, or on family errands. When my son became a teenager, the same happened to him on more than one occasion. Like other Black boys, racism marked the beginning of the denial by police officers of his everyday normal enjoyments as a teenager on his growing journey to become a young adult and a man. These Black sons learned early in life that their racial identities are deemed "less than." Their racial identities are devalued and treated without respect from white police officers. The sufferings and injustices that racism places on our children are often heavier for mothers to bear than the agony and burdens of racism on ourselves. To confront the impact of our Black children's frequent racist experience requires an ongoing process of fortifying them with strong self-esteem mechanisms that are designed to strengthen them. As mothers, we share the hard work of instilling self-esteem in our Black boys.

In the twenty-first century, mothers' fears for their Black sons have escalated to greater fears. The continuous manifestations of racism mirror the horrific history of racism long ago. We are now witnessing too many Black sons whose mothers' hopes are denied by the horrific killing of their sons by white police officers. The reality of this witness is well documented. In the highly accredited book *Breaking Rank*,[3] Norm Stamper, a white police officer, speaks volumes to the racism that dwells within police forces resulting in the death of Black males who are their mothers' Black sons. There is also the article "A Black Boy Is Dead" by Tommy J. Curry and Gwenetta D. Curry.[4] In their discussion of Trayvon Martin's death, they note the over three hundred Black people killed in 2012 and the hundreds of Black people killed by police officers every year, most of them are men and many names we do not know. Their witness to the deaths of other mothers' Black sons vis-à-vis their own Black sons spirals their fears into sorrow. Just as Black bodies were not considered human during slavery, so too is the pain experienced today for those mothers of Black sons who are not seen as human and as part of humanity. Hope of their dream deferred in favor of their Black sons is forever gone (and not simply deferred) with the killing of their Black sons by white police officers. Their sorrow is a special "kindred" sorrow, a mother's natural expectation that she would die before her Black son's life is shattered. After all, that expectation is the normal journey of life. Why not the same normality for mothers of Black sons like other mothers and their, say, white sons?

The expectation of the mothers of Black sons constantly fluctuates between hope and hopelessness of their fears and sorrows.

As Langston Hughes said in "Harlem," "What happens to a dream deferred? . . . Maybe it just sags / like a heavy load. / Or does it explode?" The hope for real freedom, equality, dignity, justice, opportunity, and success—the African American condition during the Civil Rights Movement of the 1960s—explodes for the mothers of Black sons killed by white police officers. Their hope *explodes* into slogans like *"Black Lives Matter!" and "I can't breathe!"* widely presented on placards in the ongoing protests against the death of Black sons by white police officers. Eric Garner's cry for physical help has now become a metaphor for all Blacks and especially Black mothers being choked to death by the burden of police brutality on their Black sons.

However, they are reminded that the slogan *"Black Lives Matter!"* is not acknowledged by white police officers and, indeed, has been interpreted by them as *"Black Lives (Don't) Matter!"* This problematic proposition has been held since slavery, as well as now. That explains why mothers of Black sons have realized the need to fight against such racist assumptions and to prove to white police officers that Black lives are human lives, which is embodied in the slogan *"We are Human!"* In order to respect the reality that *Black Lives Matter*, white police officers must embrace and respect our humanity. The opposition to fully acknowledging such demonstrative claims about the importance of Black humanity mattering is critically engaged in "What's Wrong with

'All Lives Matter'?" in an interview discussion between George Yancy and Judith Butler.[5]

The expectations of mothers of Black sons explode into protests that continue to hang constantly between hope and hopelessness and their joys and sorrows. The reality of their fears, sorrows, and hopes is a very agonizing burden on their hearts and minds. In moments of these mothers' leaning toward hope and not hopelessness, they realize a reservoir of strength not previously recognized. Among these strengths for me, in my personal story of fighting against racism, was recalling scholarship on racism, "which presents acid tests of my belief in humanity and simultaneously re-energizes me to persevere in the urgent need for confronting racism."[6] I also engage the public with my adopted car-tag slogan, "Color Me Human"[7] as an attempt to raise moral consciousness. Among the personal stories that appear with my story about mothers confronting racism, Martha Roth's "You Have to Start Somewhere" reminds us that perfection is not the point, rather *doing and trying* are.[8]

In these mothers' moments of leaning toward hopelessness and not hope, their perseverance wavers. Shawn R. Donaldson's "When Our Faces Are at the Bottom of the Well,"[9] also among those personal stories, shares her struggles against racism. She references Derrick Bell's position "on the profitability and permanence of racism in America."[10] Donaldson agonizes over the reality of Bell's position that full equality in this country for Blacks as a race will never be realized. Bell maintains that our herculean successes are only temporary "peaks of progress" and short-lived victories that become irrelevant as racial patterns adapt new ways to maintain white dominance. While this fact is difficult to accept, it is verified by all history.[11] The reality of Bell's position, for Donaldson, questions any hope for the future. Donaldson maintains that she "would like nothing more than to have Bell's dismal hypothesis proven wrong." [12]

Beyond the fears, sorrows, and hopes of these mothers of Black sons, there is a shared common historical thread with other mothers of Black sons in previous American eras. That common thread is the need for healing as discussed by Joy DeGruy Leary and others.[13]

Overwhelmingly, historically and now, there have been only marginal endeavors to address the devastation of the sorrows of these mothers through addressing issues of moral consciousness and social injustice—or through intervention in the form of psychological therapy. Despite the failure to adequately address the sorrows of these mothers, they still stand. As Maya Angelou would say, they indeed are "phenomenal women,"[14] and as Joy DeGruy Leary would say, they are "miracles."[15] These women, like Donaldson, come to understand not only the reality of Bell's daunting position that Black people as a group will not realize true democracy, but they will also come to realize the courage he offers. For Bell, to acknowledge this reality is not to surrender to submission, but rather to act in "ultimate defiance."[16] Donaldson notes that Bell's response is a call for continued struggle, namely "Struggle as an end rather than a means to an end, Struggle as a moral responsibility."[17] For Bell, we are obligated to work toward improving as much as possible and as many lives of Black people and other victims of injustice (including whites) as possible, and that this work "does not end because final victory over racism is unlikely, even impossible. The essence of life fulfilled—a succession of actions undertaken in righteous causes—is a victory itself."[18]

In Carl Hammerschlag's "Mussar of MLK," in honor of Martin Luther King Jr.'s birthday for 2015, he mirrors Leary's call for healing and Bell's idea of "a victory itself." Hammerschlag speaks of opening a space to the moral path in life and living one's values, being hopeful and engaging in reconciliation for healing. He urges that we share the "truth" realizing that we are not going to finish the job, but that we will leave a shining light about wisdom and the power to serve others for those who follow.[19]

21

REGARDING HENRY

T. Denean Sharpley-Whiting

"**C**raggy-faced and ornery, Edgar Ray Killen bears the signs of his 89 years. His hands are still scarred and rough from decades in the east Mississippi sawmills. He has a muscular build even as he maneuvers in his wheelchair. Time has not softened his views and he remains an ardent segregationist."[1]

The triple murders of civil rights activists, James Chaney, Andrew Goodman, and Michael Schwerner in Mississippi in 1964 and the man, Edgar Ray Killen, a Klansman working with law enforcement, who turned a violent lynch mob on the unsuspecting Freedom Riders, is as good a place as any to begin a rumination on white violence, the ways in which white supremacy impinges and intrudes in the most tragic ways upon the lives of ordinary people doing (extra)ordinary things. It provides an on-ramp into a tumultuous history whose grisly throughway, strewn with mangled black bodies, legal and extra-legal white violence, and despairing and exasperating caws of white innocence, many believed had been discontinued instead of rerouted into our present moment of brazen, state-sanctioned, and predominantly white male violence.

Killen's story ends most ironically—in Parchman Prison in Mississippi, a correctional facility notorious for its warehousing of black men on all and sundry offenses. He formed an easy friendship with a nonviolent offender named James Stern for protection over the course of a year and a half. Stern was serving time on seven counts of wire-fraud charges. Newly freed, in 2012, Stern had in his possession the power of attorney and land rights for forty acres of Killen's land in Mississippi. Stern in turn transferred the land to a nonprofit he controls called, "Racial Reconciliation," and deeded one acre of the land for a memorial site to the three slain civil rights workers. In defending the authenticity of the signed documents, Stern protested, "When they were putting feces in his food, I was the one giving him my tray."[2] Stern also said Killen admitted to scores of other murders of blacks. He invited the government to begin exploratory digging on the land: "I spent one and a half years housed with Edgar Ray Killen, as I told you, he's confessed to many things, even his wife in phone conversations spoke to me of bush hogging the property, many days of covering up things in the pastures."[3]

I begin with this bit of history—which occurred in the backwater town of Philadelphia, Mississippi, that inspired a Hollywood movie, *Mississippi Burning* and that served in reckless disregard of that terrible history as the launch site of Ronald Reagan's presidential campaign—because in 2014 Killen granted his first interview in the nine years since his conviction in 2005. A staunch but practical segregationist, given his reliance on Stern for protection, the hot glare of the media spotlight on Killen allows us to make connections between policing, terror, white innocence and lack of empathy, and black males, between the mourners left in the detritus of white insouciance and apathy with respect to black male lives and black mothers' pain.

The prescient understanding of Schwerner's widow, Rita Bender, a field officer for the Congress of Racial Equality (C.O.R.E.) and participant in Freedom Summer, about the cheapness of black life in America rings as true now, some five decades later, as it did then in 1964. The national outrage, media, and immediacy around the case were a consequence of the disappearance of two white men: "If he and Andrew Goodman had been Negroes, the world would have taken little notice of their deaths. After all, the slaying of a Negro in Mississippi is not news. It is only because my husband and Andrew Goodman were white that the national alarm has been sounded."[4] And certainly the autopsies revealed the particular torture meted out to Chaney—a chain beating and three gunshot wounds—as a consequence of his blackness and daring to defy the protocols of white supremacy held sacrosanct by the murderous, marauding band of white male perpetrators.

But I'd like to now turn to a rumination on gendered, white racist violence and how it trespassed upon black family matters in the most intimate of ways in the 1920s such that its reverberations continue to be felt in this new millennium; it is a history of middle-class strivers and respectability. *My family's history.* Perhaps differing from the more contemporary entries in this anthology because it is, one, historical, and, two, I am not a black mother who lives daily with the fear of white racial violence against her son, this essay resonates for it is the story of a black mother and son, who, conceived in the spectral of gendered racial violence, reels from the trauma of said violence and is forever lost to the family who made him and the family he made. White racism and its consequences are then like hauntings that seep and sweep through generations.

My grandmother was a rape survivor. She was a teenager with dreams of becoming an opera singer like Lillian "Evanti" Evans-Tibbs. Her perpetrator came from that privileged class of white men who had taken the Hippocratic oath. Her illness was a common cold whose persistence caused my great-grandmother, her mother, a dressmaker who owned a shop that occupied the front section of their home, great concern. The doctor was a man who they, my great-grandmother and her four pretty, sheltered daughters, had come to trust. These were the days when doctors called at patients' homes. The nameless doctor assaulted my grandmother, while her mother busied herself with fabrics, patterns, and prints in her storefront dress shop. When I was told the story, I imagined my great-grand riffling through pretty things, tulle and silk, oblivious to the ugliness occurring in the living quarters of her own home.

The rape set in motion an industrious cover-up and family silences; though my grandmother talked openly, defiantly even, about the rape and the rapist (nameless though he remained, as if to name him would conjure him up in the flesh)—the consequences—conception and illegitimacy—engendered waves of melancholia for dreams clipped and an eventual family rupture.

There were no *A Time to Kill/Bush Mama*–style reenactments. My grandmother's half-Irish father was long dead. My great-grandmother, who'd remarried, and my grandmother set about righting the wrong in their own wily way. Unwilling to bring the doctor to justice as it would expose my grandmother's despoiling as it were, they proceeded to hide

the pregnancy through various styles of dress—after all my great-grand
was a seamstress—and contrived it as my great-grand's late-in-life pregnancy. Henry, as the child was named, was then promptly given my
great-grandmother's second husband's last name.

With the threat to their good name averted, my grandmother eventually married my caramel-colored grandfather. Swaddled in the legitimacy of the matrimonial bed, my father—the brown prince of my
great-grandmother's dreams—was born when my grandmother was
thirty-six years old. In him, outings to the opera, museums, and restaurants were poured as they had been for Henry decades before. The
wayward elder brother, though, preferred jazz and deftly played a trum-
pet. These recollections are my father's earliest fleeting memories of his
brother. Two other reminisces, more telling, would follow.

Against this backdrop of striving despite adversity, intra-racial con-
flicts around color and class also engulfed my family. Some vocal members of their black community, particularly those who were willing to
recognize these straight-, raven-haired, milk-colored women as what
they said they were—black, could not understand why women who
could pass for white and never, ever, look back, did not. And my great-
grandmother, puffed up with middle-class affectations and pretentions,
was also quick to dismiss those who were "not our class, dear." Their
world was divided into creators and takers, readers and the ignorant,
the well mannered and the uncouth. They lived under scrutiny in their
segregated St. Louis community. Everything about them seemed suspicious; who they married, what they wore—a mark of their uppityness—
and so much so that an unbalanced neighbor barked loudly in front of
their home about my grandmother, who had subsequently borne three
other children whose colors ranged from yogurt with a spoonful of
honey to piss yellow to hazel, "having half-breed babies."

Meanwhile, Henry had already begun to float to the margins of
family memories. His life was like a highlight reel: tours in the USO
(United Service Organization) as a trumpeter, a wedding, two sons, an
acrimonious split with a cantankerous wife who would later deny the
children access to their paternal relatives. Henry had abandoned them,
so the wife, in turn, punished my grandmother. Then Henry did something else. Or maybe, Henry *was* something else. The grandmothers
again never said; his erring was some unspeakable thing unspoken,[5] and
quiet as it's kept, conjecture about a defect passed on from his base

white father, for only a defective man would rape, hung in the air accusatorily. Henry's long fall down became attributed to an almost Emile Zolaesque naturalism and degeneration. When a knock on the door from a white stranger bearing the authority of the Veteran's Administration inquired if Henry could return home, he was turned out and away. These women had outwitted one outrage. They wouldn't dare open the door willingly to another—whatever the blood bond. At least that's the standard to which my upright, great-grand held the family line.

My grandmother in the meantime continued to clandestinely search out her son and the family he'd left behind: letters to the Veteran's Administration, tracking the last known address of her grandsons and their remarried mother. These facts wouldn't be known until well after my great-grandmother's death. My grandmother revered, and yet, had cleverly defied her strong-willed mother who'd lived for ninety-something years. Pictures of my grandmother with a pretty, teenage girl surfaced. We came to understand that these pictures were taken under the most covert of circumstances. A neighbor who was also a parishioner at my grandmother's church allowed the two, my grandmother and her great-granddaughter, to meet at her home. Gifts were surreptitiously passed. Hugs were exchanged. A breakthrough. My grandmother shared the news with her daughter. Then the meetings and gifts were discovered, and the girl told my grandmother and aunt she had no paternal great-grandmother or aunt. Though Henry had somehow rent apart his created family, they still loved him as only the abandoned can love the missing, weaving alternate narratives and realities, and simultaneously hated him and hated my grandmother and therefore us—the ones who remained secreted tenderly in the bosom of maternal bonds. Only once the two sides met, Henry's and his siblings' children. The understandable bitterness about abandonment and rejection suspiciously tied to the difference manifest in the original sin simmered just beneath the brief rapprochement.

There was very little consolation to be had in the fact that my grandmother deeply mourned the loss of her eldest son whose violent conception in the maelstrom of white supremacy marked them both in different ways, regretted that she had allowed her mother and concerns about propriety to disrupt the bond by turning him away when he needed her most. But she had to be responsible for and protect the other four charges in her care.[6] There was, though, a collective recognition of my grandmother's violation at the hands of a sexually violent and predatory white man. There was very limited legal recourse for women to prosecute rape in 1920s America. There was no legal recourse for the rape of a black woman in 1920s America against a seemingly upstanding white man. And sadly, there was no recovery—even after my grandmother's heroic recovery from that traumatic violence—for our sundered family. The intervening years were too vast to recover and the hurts had congealed on one side.

There is a black-and-white photo of my uncle among my grandmother's personal effects. Taken in the 1940s, he is handsome, tall, lean, and nattily dressed in a sports coat. He smiles easily into the camera, carefree as only a young man in his twenties might be. The photograph is all that remains of my grandmother's eldest son. It is of Henry before he became a "free man," in the Morrisonian sense, "with nothing more to lose" and only "his own perceptions and appetites and they alone interested him."[7]

NOTE

The title of this chapter is drawn from the 1991 film, *Regarding Henry*, starring Harrison Ford. I'd like to thank my father, Muriel Sharpley, his sister and my aunt Sharon and my cousin Anita for their various recollections that helped to inform this essay.

III

Poems

22

A LOVE POEM FOR MICHAEL BROWN

Elisheba Johnson

My tears aren't going to save my black son.
And my fears aren't a shield either.
I was living in a false reality believing my love was a bullet proof vest.
Sybrina loved Trayvon.
She loved him every moment that he was stalked and then murdered.
Lesley loved Michael.
She loved him every moment of those four hours his body lay on the concrete
bleeding,
Dead.
They love their boys.
And I love my son.
Our love has to be enough.
My love isn't a bullet proof vest.
But I wish it was.
A mother's love is a unique beautiful gift.
It is unmatched,
It is everything,
It is pervasive.
And in the morning when I dress him
I kiss his cheek
And tell him I love him
As if that is all he needs
To fend off the evils of the world.
How naïve am I?

In those moments I believe my love can penetrate hate.
That the same love that deals with a two year old's tantrums,
Can stop a cop from throwing him against a police car.
That the same love that kisses his owies,
Can stop his teachers from suspending him without due cause
That the same love that shows up after a long day at work and still
reads a good night story,
Can stop a woman from falsely accusing him of a crime.
That same love that tucks him into bed,
Can stop him from being murdered and the media spinning it into
character assassination.
All that love.
The love that I restore and keep giving.
The love that is endless.
My love must be so strong that it can stop anyone
Killing a child I spent my days breathing life into.
My love isn't a bullet proof vest.
But it is endless.
Us mothers,
We love our children from the moment they are conceived.
Sybrina loves Trayvon.
Lesley loves Michael.
I love Emery.
My tears aren't going to save my black son.
And my fears aren't a shield either.
My love isn't a bullet proof vest.
But my love is endless
And that is more than enough.

23

LAMENTATIONS FROM A BLACK MOM

Dyan Watson

Dear Caleb and Nehemiah,
Last night I wept because of you, my black sons.
It wasn't the first time I cried over you.

Caleb, I cried the first time I heard about you ---
I'm going to have a boy!
I cried the first time I saw you ----
Big, dark, handsome.
My boy, my son.
My black son.

Today, my black son, I cry again.
I cry because you are
big, dark, handsome.
You are Mike Brown and Eric Garner.
You are gregarious and passionate.
You laugh with your entire body and when you're angry, your dimples deepen.
You are cute and still have cheeks that everyone wants to pinch.
But one day you will grow
and some police officer might see you as a monster
some woman might clutch her purse when you walk by.

You will remind some of what they hate in themselves.
So today I cry.

Nehemiah, I cried just moments after you arrived in this world,
as they swept you away to NICU
and worked to free your lungs of the water that had gathered there.
Today, my black son, I cry again.
I cry because you are light skinned and have "good" hair.
You are Trayvon Martin.
You are quick witted and watchful.
You raise one eyebrow when you're seeking to understand something.
You love to be thrown up in the air and to ask "Why, Mommy? Why?"
But one day you will grow
and remind them that you don't really belong and how they have
failed you but how they don't want to change.
So today I cry.

Sons, don't bring me tears.
Don't carry fake guns,
untaxed cigarettes,
or Skittles.
Keep your hands out of your pockets
and stay out of their neighborhoods.

Don't make me cry.
Stay alive. Don't die before
I do.

24

FOR TRAYVON

Treasure Shields Redmond

when we are born the color of smoke,
or wood, or butter, or honey
or cotton.

when are born natural with a green
mark at the base of our spine. uncircumcised,
carrying generations in sacks inside us.

when we are born black and alive looking
like a long dead great grandfather; right
then an invisible stopwatch starts.
—milliseconds count as hours
when your black boy life is only a coda
in the paragraph, & it takes ten
thousand of your muscled bodies to stand
for africa in a film, but only one of you
dead to stand for America.

you were once a red lump of clay
inside this fearful womb, an idea
about freedom, a ditty that became a song,
a graduation photo,
a boy,
a baby.
born black and alive, an unfinished poem
about lynching

a body,
a potential,
a body.
dark nipples, rough knees,
a body.
baby toes, crooked,
a body.
a curved back
a body.
earlobes,
a body.
lies buried
in a southern town
again.
not this body.
not here.
not in this nice neighborhood.

not a black boy body
moving free and alive.

in america your black boy body
offends/offender/capital offense
against your black body.
be still,
or behind steel,
or pierced by steel.
but why can't a black boy born alive stay that way?

25

NEWS OF YOU, MY SON

Sharyn Skeeter

[One]

In His Dark Room

I want his noise.
I want his sneakers
squish, squishing in his room.
I want his speaker
thump, thumping, and his
young man voice sweet
whispering of babies
and weddings to Cassie
on his phone.

My son is coming home.
I know he is.
I know that man-lump
blanketed and bloody in the street
was not him. I know
the scream I heard was not me.

I cannot stand the quiet.
My panting echoes on the walls.
I rattle the dishes,
shatter a glass,
sizzle cheese on macaroni.
It sputters, burnt, when it overflows.

My boy's coming home.
He'll traipse his muddy shoes
down the hall I just mopped.
His key will catch in
the lock, soon, I know.

[Two]

His Face in Cracked Glass

This robot-faced cop woman says
"I am sorry for your loss."
Her words are computer
keys peeling my nails.

"We don't know who did this."
Her badge-bosom heaves
in my face. She doesn't see
his photos, their frames twisted,
cracked glass on the floor.
My bare toes are bloody,
smudging him there
    yearbook grin
      prom tux with Cassie
      basketball hero, my son.
Why did you leave me?

"We'll keep his file open."
My son, my son is not a file.
His heart is splayed wide
open and raw like turkey
gizzards, liver for a dog.

"We will be in touch."
I bend to his crumpled
six-year-old eyes, watching me
pick up chips. I hold tight, do not
feel them flaying my fist. I want
to throw glass in her face. She
catches my wrist. Her fingers, pale
icepicks, spike through my bone.

[Three]

How Did He Get in a Box?

How did I get to this church
where my son is altar-ready,
suit, tie, clean shaven,
boxed in satin and oak?
Oh, the sight of him!
His brown skin powdered gray,
plaster cheek hides the bullet,
blasted hands in gloves I knitted.
Where Cassie wants to kiss
his chin he'd fall apart,
as I am. How did I get in this pew
where his daddy's eyes are heavy,
his forehead buried in my shoulders?

If only I had listened when
my son told me of missions
to Mars, of championships,
and Cassie.
But I fussed with the microwave,
ironed shirts for work, fried
chicken in the skillet.

If only his daddy had talked
to him at dinner. He yelled
our boy's chores over sitcoms and
through the crack in his bedroom door.

If only Cassie's belly
wasn't round. If only
he had not been near
that boy who robbed the deli,
who had the gun, who shot.
If only the cops had stopped.

[Four]

As I Walk Through the Aisle

Store clerks don't smile anymore
when I walk through the bread aisle.
They've seen news of you—
my son, shot dead.
They see my headphones,
hear me sing to myself,
to your tenor in my ears,
    "and when I'm feeling lonely,
     I hear music in the air."
They look down, unpack boxes,
let me pass at their backs.

Your hymn is all I can
hear of you. You are with me.
Your grocery list is a prayer,
sacred and sweaty in my palm.
I reach for your chips, then
remember you're gone.
My cart is empty at checkout.

Last time we were here I
forgot your blueberries for
Sunday muffins. Your choir voice
vibrates my skull. The woman
behind me pushes vitamin
water on the counter, wants
me to leave. I run
to get berries and flour,
I sing with you,
bake for you.

[Five]

Grandson Needs Changing

Cassie's baby closes
his fist around my finger.

His soft pulse is fast,
mine slow. In the split-
second between beats, I
glance at the photo of my son,
smiling, next to his crib.

You, my son, are the spasm
that gave this boy life,
quick as the bullet
that took yours.
He is a feather on my chest.
His brown eyes
are yours. His tiny arms
waving at me, hers.

He's wet. My hands still have
the habit of diaper's folds.
I don't have time to remember
me, sitting on my son's bed
in the dark. Baby is hungry.
It's 5:30. Cassie will be home.
He needs her milk.

26

DEATH PASSES TWICE

Autumn Redcross

They say that death passes around the bed twice,
When you're in labor.
My mother told me this.
The logic of the tale gives hint to the gravity of childbirth—
The risk and the frailty of the lives involved.
Death, as a ghost, circles
At first taunting to take the mother with;
Death then comes around again
For the chance to take the soul of the newborn.

Babies are born every day
With no serious consequence;
However, some are lost.
My first living birth was a girl.
Disappointed as I was by the
Misstep in my "ideal" birth order
My mother's words encouraged me,
"You'll be glad that you had a girl first," she said.
And I am.

Two years later, I got my boy
Shortly after that, my third, another male was born
Three babes in all! I count my lucky stars.
As if a prophet, my mother spoke truth about having my girl first

Maternal instincts intact, she cares for us all;
She looks out for her brothers, most.
Yet, I cannot help but to reflect on the act
Of giving birth to, and bringing up, black boys
As an encircling encounter with death itself.

Contorted during labor
And bearing down hard to deliver
I give birth to this being,
An image of God
And of my own body's making.
Flesh of my flesh,
He is not simply a baby; he is a black baby boy.
A man child;
A threat.

Epidermal encasing
Proceeding his being;
He will never know different.
His mirrored reflection
Is not what they see;
Instead, his identity is painted
By the brush strokes of others.
A body not wholly his own,
He must navigate from this unyielding cast.

Me, I hold my breath; I guard our hearts;
We dare to live despite what has become *commonsensical.*
In this historic moment, our black sons can be beaten,
Maimed, shot and left for dead—
To no serious consequence for the murderous.
Bureaucracy offering too few indictments,
Little apology and no regret
Leaving us mothers to mourn our loss unto our bodies, ourselves.
And what do we have, if what we have, what we are, and what we bare,
is ungrievable?

These days,
As each day
Starts with the morning,
Mourning starts
Before the life begins.
The ghost of death passes twice
When you're in labor.
As a mother of black boys
I feel its presence still.

It ebbs, it flows this labor
That is my daily life—
Mothering black boys.
Death passes first
Taking pieces of hope—
The kind of hope mothers of others could afford.
Death circles around again
Leaving a dehumanizing legacy
Of the black baby boy in its wake.

IV

Letters

27

DEAR WILLIAM

Gretchen Givens Generett

This is not a small love
you hear this is a large
love, a longing to know why Love
at this exact moment Love.
This is a love that surrenders to risking it all
For different outcomes, different results that saves lives Love
That opens hearts instead of settling for unjust norms Love
where we no longer cry in our cars with windows up and behind our
children's backs Love.
This is a love that says no more.
This is a love that says no more.
—Inspired by the poem, *This Is Not a Small Voice* by Sonia Sanchez,
Beacon Press, 1999

Dear William,
I started this piece more times than I care to mention. The heaviness of thinking about what I would say and how I would say it has manifested in many forms of busying myself. Any excuse was a reason not to write because the excuses allowed me to push down the anger, fear, frustration, anxiety, sadness, and bile taste that wells up in my being when I hear or see yet another Black man shot, killed, and beaten by the police. This letter has been hard, very hard because I have not wanted to sit still long enough to gather my "logical" thoughts about why we are having to, at this moment and time, deal with police killing our boys. Indeed, I am more like my mother's mother and her mother's mother

now than ever. Despite having ancestors who survived slavery and worked to dismantle Jim Crow laws, despite having earned a doctorate, tenure, financial security, health coverage—name all the things that define my life as privileged—I am just like all the Black mothers who came before me. Blessed and cursed with the profoundly awesome task of raising a Black male child in a country that continues to question the humanness and humanity of Black men. Therein lies why it is so difficult to find the words.

How could they not see your humanity? You? My dear, sweet child.

You have heard this before, but I chose the academy because I was thirsty for stories of success about Black people in education. I wanted to read more of them, so I decided to research and write them. My desire to do research in education that included the educational stories of African Americans came from this overwhelming feeling that this country did not believe that excellence, education, and Black were synonymous. This is not unusual. Most people do not know or care to know the stories of everyday African Americans like your grandparents and great-grandparents. Most people do not care that the stories of people like your family are the very essence of American values, strength, and courage. Indeed, their sacrifices made the life I live today, and the life your father and I are able to afford you, possible. Telling their stories makes them real, more visible. Telling their stories allows others to see and better understand how what they did was like nutrients poured into me. The rich sustenance of heritage and culture from being in their presence made me believe that I could do whatever I set my mind to. I could do anything because I was an extension of them and they were survivors in trying times. I tell you the stories of my growing up with three generations of family because being tethered to my grandmother's porch let me know that I was loved. Being on that porch was where my humanity was confirmed. My storytelling is my attempt to tether you to that same porch, that same sense of self. The comfort is in knowing that you are not alone. Such love affirms your right to claim your space wherever you go because of the sacrifices your ancestors made for you.

Does that make sense? I sure hope so.

I would like to believe that if we knew more about each other's stories, about how we are loved by our families, then we would have less killing of us by them. I would like to think that we would become more visible to each other. I would like to think that they could imagine what it might feel like to have a mother, like me, lose a son like you because someone thought that you were a monster instead of my dear, sweet child. I would like to think that just the thought of such a loss would propel them into action, into doing something so that such an awful thing could never happen again. I would like to think that because they could imagine my heartbreak from the loss of my son, their visceral response would be to learn how white supremacy and institutionalized racism has gotten us here. And that, indeed, this is nothing new. More than forty years ago, Ella Baker's response to the disappearance of one Black and two white Civil Rights workers in Mississippi, gave pause. She said,

> Until the killings of Black men, Black mothers' sons, becomes as important to the rest of the country as the killings of a white mother's son, we who believe in freedom cannot rest until this happens.[1]

Her comments expressed her anger and frustration upon learning that when search crews searched local rivers and swamps, the bodies of other Black men who did not have the benefit of an organized search were discovered. It was as if they did not matter.

Black mothers have been screaming for years that their children's lives matter.

I saw a white woman the other day and she was wearing a t-shirt that said, "ALL Lives Matter." I cringed. Why? Because my work with white educators tells me that their colorblind ideology will continue to produce racist and prejudice students who, like many of their teachers, associate Blackness with something negative. Think about it, the only reason to not see something clearly in front of your face is if there is something "wrong" with it or it reminds you of something you would rather not see. They do not want to see Blackness because then they would have to acknowledge that they associate Blackness with low grades, bad behavior, poor choices. They would have to acknowledge that they associate Blackness with deficit, thug, perpetrator, guilty. If you associate Blackness with goodness, why would you not want to see it?

Black, youth, asset, love, innocent.

On December 4, 2014, in response to police brutality, *The Progressive* magazine reprinted one of James Baldwin's most famous pieces. It is entitled, "A Letter to My Nephew," and it was first published in 1962. You must read the entire letter, but I pulled out a small part of it so that you would understand why your teachers would rather claim to be colorblind than to see that you are a Black boy. James Baldwin writes to his nephew:

> Many of them indeed know better, but as you will discover, people find it very difficult to act on what they know. To act is to be committed and to be committed is to be in danger. In this case the danger in the minds and hearts of most white Americans is the loss of their identity. Try to imagine how you would feel if you woke up one morning to find the sun shivering and all the stars aflame. You would be frightened because it is out of the order of nature. Any upheaval in the universe is terrifying because it so profoundly attacks one's sense of one's own reality. Well, the black man has functioned in the white man's world as a fixed star, as an immovable pillar, and as he moves out of his place, heaven and earth are shaken to their foundations.[2]

If white people's identity is tied to Black men being fixed stars that cannot move out of place, then the stories white people tell about themselves and, most importantly, about Black men have got to change. They have to unlearn and relearn American history in a way that is inclusive of all the people of color who helped to build this country. They have to examine how the institutions they have created are designed to get outcomes that, decade after decade, reproduce inequitable and unjust results for people of color, women, and those living in poverty. All systems are perfectly designed to get the outcomes they produce. They have to acknowledge that the deficit is fixed within the system, not innate to a race of people. They have to look at how institutional racism is tearing at the very core of this country. And how it is a huge waste of finances and talent—think about the school-to-prison pipeline. It is far cheaper to educate people than to put them in prison. What a waste of money and talent! As Dr. King has already taught us, regardless of racial affiliation, all of humanity is "caught in an inescapable network of mutuality, tied in a single garment of destiny."[3] They must be honest about how their need to privilege a few keeps this country from reaching its highest potential. They have to be committed to the ideals they espouse.

So, how do we get there? How do we become visible to them? How do we get to a place where, indeed, ALL LIVES really do matter?

Do you remember the day we were in the park and a little boy hit and pushed you down? You were six years old. You were so upset. You could not understand why he would do something like that to you. After all, you had not done anything to him, as you explained through your tears. As I tried to console you, I gave you permission to defend yourself; that if someone put their hands on you, you had a right to hit back. At the wise old age of six, you said to me, "That is not me. I want to use my words." My dear, sweet child. My dear, sweet, innocent child. You named who you were at that young age. In that moment, you claimed your space by telling me who you are. You did not allow me to tell you who you had to be. "That is not me." Your exact words!

I think we get there, William, by being who we know we are and not who they say we are. We get there by continuing to love despite their dishonesty, even when we are hurt, outraged, and sad. Why, you ask? Because you come from ancestors who sacrificed so much. They all, we all, are pouring the essence of love, hope, and spirit into you. You, and the young Black men of your generation, are our hope. But most importantly, William, you are their only hope. They have no chance of getting *there* without you leading and showing them the way.

28

A LETTER TO CJ

Regina Sims Wright

June 22, 2015

Dear CJ,

At the age of thirty-six, I gave birth to you. I had nearly given up on having a family and never expected that you would arrive just ten months after your dad and I were married. Now I am a mother—the mother of a Black boy—and I have a lot of concerns about your future. Let me share with you some of the events that have taken place and some of the feelings that I've had surrounding your arrival.

On February 6, 2012, an unarmed seventeen-year-old boy named Trayvon Martin was senselessly killed in Sanford, Florida, while walking through a gated community, after returning from a store for some candy and juice. It took some time for the case to reach the national spotlight, but when it did, people of color all over the country were in an uproar. Eventually, the man who killed Trayvon was charged, but later acquitted of the killing, and again the country was in an uproar. During that time, I was a relatively new professor at my university. Like many others, I was angry about the lack of justice for Trayvon. I participated in a rally on campus and voiced my concerns over social media and among my family and friends. I was sad for Trayvon's family and could not understand how a seemingly open-and-shut case led to no punishment for a man who stalked and killed a young boy. My heart was broken, but the pain faded over time. I was not yet a mother.

Just over two years later, an unarmed twenty-year-old man named Michael Brown was shot and killed in Ferguson, Missouri, after being stopped by a cop for walking in the middle of the street. The police tried to portray Michael as a suspect in a robbery shortly after, but it became clear that the officer was unaware of that robbery when he pursued Michael. The accounts of the scuffle that took place were sketchy, but in the end, Michael lay dead on the ground for hours. This time, the outcry was huge, and community organizers and people from all over demanded justice for Michael Brown. Sadly, the officer was not indicted by the Ferguson, Missouri, court system and later the Department of Justice found there was no evidence of a civil rights violation. At this time, I was about three months pregnant. As the Ferguson riots went on and the nation was divided about the role of racism in Michael Brown's shooting, I found out that I was having a boy. Within months, Eric Garner, suspected of selling cigarettes illegally, was choked and killed, John Crawford III was shot after walking through Walmart with an air rifle, and Tamir Rice was shot and killed after waving a toy gun around in the park—all at the hands of police.

Just two years earlier, I was childless and focused almost entirely on my career. Now I was preparing for your birth. I was terrified. I felt the weight of the world on my shoulders as I anticipated the immense responsibility of raising you right, and the reality that raising you right just might not be enough. It seemed as though every month the news was reporting another Black boy or man being snuffed out—never armed, but always considered dangerous. The youngest of those victims, Tamir Rice, finally brought me to tears. I realized then that I was living in a society where even a twelve-year-old was not immune to being feared by others and faced severe consequences for being a kid while Black.

At the heart of all of these issues was racism. Since slavery, many White men and women have feared the very individuals they oppressed. Thus, Black people in the United States have always experienced double jeopardy. We are discriminated against and misunderstood for being Black, and ultimately mistreated for the fear, shame, and guilt that our oppressors feel at the hands of their own wrongdoing. Many people consider

2015 to represent a post-racial America, but there are countless examples of overt racism in the media each day. I believe our nation is no less racist than it was fifty years ago; the recent outward characteristics of racism in America have just shifted. Our arrest and conviction policies, prison populations, employment and housing opportunities, and educational quality reflect a very racist United States. We have a long way to go.

Aside from racism, many Blacks and Whites have been discussing how Black-on-Black crime is rampant and that it's no surprise that Black men are seen as threatening. These conversations suggest that Black men deserve what they have coming to them since they don't respect and kill one another. I want you to know that all human life is valuable, and no one has the right to make a judgment about whether someone deserves to live or die, especially by looking at his or her skin tone. Yes, some Black men are violent and have killed. The media will trick you, though, into believing that these kinds of men are everywhere. It's just not true. There are many more Black men respecting their fellow man, working hard, raising their families, and being good citizens. Your dad is one of them and you will be, too.

As I thought about your future in the wake of so many tragedies, I wondered how I could protect you when I had so many examples that showed you would be devalued and feared as a Black man. So many ideas bounced around in my head. I told your dad that we should move to Canada. I was sure I could get a faculty position there. They treat Black men better there. We talked about moving to a few other countries, but the reality was that we weren't going anywhere. Then I began to think about how I could groom you so that you would appear "non-threatening." How could I dress you? What kind of haircut could you have? How could we keep the attention away from you? Your dad is not a big man. I wondered if your frame would be small and help you to appear non-threatening. I also began thinking about how we could groom your behavior so that you wouldn't attract trouble. Then I thought about Trayvon and Tamir, both of whom were well behaved. Being a good kid did not protect them from a horrible fate. Despite all of these concerns, your dad and I are working very hard to ensure that you can grow up in a decent neighborhood and go to excellent schools.

The challenge is that the better the neighborhood or the better the school, the more you might be perceived as an outsider. Trayvon's father was visiting his fiancée in a really nice neighborhood when Trayvon was killed. In fact, Trayvon's very presence as a Black boy in that gated community led to his demise.

As you can see, CJ, there are no good answers for how to protect you. It is my intent as your mother to lay a foundation that will help to keep you safe. In the end, all we can do is surrender your protection to God and educate you about the reality of how the world may view you. You are warm and loving, but one day the world will fear you. You must be warm and loving anyway. It will be up to them to make the right choices. I pray that the grace of God keeps you whole and out of harm's way.

Love Always,
Mom

29

KILLING/SAVING/LOVING BLACK BOYS

Karsonya Wise Whitehead

Dear boys:

I would like to write you a love letter about peace/ of a time when black men, like black panthers, roamed free/ of a place where black bodies were not endangered and black life was not criminalized.

Alas, I am not old enough to remember life back that far (if it ever even existed in this country).

Neither am I old enough to remember life before Brown.

I suspect (though) that it was not much different than it is now in places like Ferguson and New York and Florida/ places across America where the crime of breathing while black is still punishable by death.

I used to be afraid of white sheets (wouldn't even use them on my bed) till folks traded them in for blue uniforms/ and then traded their wooden crosses in for billy clubs.

My heart always skips a beat when a cop's car is behind me while I'm driving at night/ and though you are not old enough to drive, I am already frightened by the day when you are stopped for the crime of driving while black.

There are days when being black in America overwhelms me and makes me want to spend the day in bed/ and times when being the black mother of black boys in America makes me wish I had enough money to move you somewhere where I could keep you safe.

Safe from them—the ones who see your life as expendable and unnecessary/ and from us—those who look at you without realizing that you are a mirror that simply reflects them.

I often think about slavery and how different life was when you could see the hand that held the chain that was attached to the ball that was tied to your ankle.
We come from a people who experienced this daily and still chose to survive.
Survival is our legacy.
And since we survived the Middle Passage as involuntary passengers on a trip that sealed our fate/ And we survived slavery, whips and lashes by learning how to give way and stay small/ And we survived the Civil War by claiming freedom at the hands of those who looked like our oppressors
—surviving is our goal.

We are a long-willed stubborn people.
Who survived sharecropping and the period called the nadir,
The Great Depression, Vietnam, Reaganomics, and crack cocaine.

We are a stubborn and strong-willed people.
Who survived lynchings, cross burnings, and being terrorized for wanting to vote and for trying to reclaim our voices.

We who have been beaten and starved,
Disenfranchised and disempowered,
Overlooked and ignored,
Underpaid and underrepresented.
But
We survived because we are strong-willed and stubborn.
And though there are times when we are like strangers in a foreign land/ we look around and wonder how we got here/ we take stock and realize how little we actually have/ we wonder how long we will continue to suffer and die at the hands of both the oppressor and of the oppressed
—we survive anyway.
Because survival is our legacy.
There are days when I look at the two of you and my heart swells with pride
As I think about all that you used to be and all that you can become,

And then I stop and catch my breath/ I grab my chest and clutch my pearls/
I blink back tears and shake my head/ thinking about the lives of every mother of every unarmed black boy who has died kneeling at the feet of a racist system where guilty verdicts are meted out
—one chokehold at a time
—one gunshot at a time
—one lynching at a time
—one whipping at a time.
I think of these boys daily (what black mother of black boys doesn't)
I try to speak their names/ going back as far as I can remember/ adding new names daily.
I do it so that I can remember/ so that the two of you can't forget/ so that together we can add their names and their lives to the wind so that a piece of them and this moment will remain at this place/ even though we will move on.
There are nights when I stand in the doorway of your room—not to wake you up for the revolution but to simply remind myself that, just for a moment, you are still safe and still here.
All I want (at this moment) is what every other mother wants around the world—the
simple comfort of knowing that the lives of my sons do matter and that my work—to pour love, light, and truth into them, will not be in vain.
I move from being upset and hurt to being angry and infuriated: because from skittles to hoodies, loud rap music to cigarillos, toy guns to iced tea; whether you are 18 or 12(!), college bound or not, a homeboy or a choir boy, hands held up or down on your knees, walking in the street or standing in Walmart, during the day or at night, in Ohio or in Florida or in Baltimore ~ you two are Not SAFE in this country.
As your very angry mother, I cannot and will not rest until that truth/ that sad reality has been changed.
We are survivors.
We are stubborn.
We are strong-willed.
Survival is our legacy and surviving everyday—in this system—is our goal.
There will come a day when you will know what it means to be free/ what it means to be safe/what is means to be.

I look forward to being there with you, on the dawn of this new day, and to celebrating with you.

Until . . .

Mom

NOTE

A version of this letter originally appeared in Whitehead's *Letters to My Black Sons: Raising Boys in a Post-Racial America* (Baltimore, MD: Apprentice House, 2015).

30

ANGER

Jacki Lynn Baynks

Son, I'm angry.

It's not a medical secret in terms of what anger can do to your body. Anger that is not released can kill you through sickness. I've heard you preach on it from the pulpit. It will give you high blood pressure, cause strokes, heart attacks, and all kinds of ailments. I know this and suffer from high blood pressure. My doctor says the culprit is my diet, salt intake. But I know better. It's because I'm angry.

I'm angry because I can't vent about black sons being targets. Instead I have to remain noncommittal as my white coworkers give their opinions on why Walter Scott was shot or tsk tsk as "terrible" the death of Trayvon Martin and while they wonder aloud why did violence erupt in Baltimore in 2015 as though we're back in the "prehistoric" days of Rodney King?

I'm angry because they think that their view is perfectly valid in comparing Freddie Gray's abuse to their own sons being jumped and beaten unfairly by other white boys. To them, the fact that this negligent abuse was at the hands of police is a minor detail. After all, we're sharing our frustration—we're all outraged together, aren't we? White sons get beat up, too.

I'm angry because I can't really tell them how stupid that sounds without hurting their feelings. They're nice people, but clueless regarding the impact blaming the victim in my presence is having on my blood pressure. "He shouldn't have run," they say. "You should never run. If you didn't do anything why would you run from the police?" Why indeed. I nod and hold my anger in because I know they could not begin to understand why a black man would not trust the police to not frame, beat, maim, or kill him after a traffic stop.

I'm angry because I can't say how I really feel (and get release) because then I would scare my coworkers. They see me as a non-threatening nice black woman. They feel free to engage in this conversation because I'm not considered "ghetto" or "volatile." I'm civilized to them, especially as I speak "proper" English, not the YouTube, "ain't nobody got time for that" Internet phrase they gleefully ridicule that reinforces their stereotypes of black people.

I'm angry because they expect me to laugh with them, and at times I have been weak enough to do so. "I'm just saying."

I'm angry because you, my son, have shared with me your viewpoint of "He shouldn't have run" and "He was in the wrong place at the wrong time."

I'm angry because you really believe that this could never happen to you because you obey the law and don't go to bars, because you live in the suburbs next to white people and go to the Monroeville mall early in the day because as you put it, "the niggas come out at night and you have less chance of being mistaken for one."

I'm angry because you have bought into the lie that white people don't see you as a nigger because your pants don't sag, you sound "educated," and you have white friends.

I'm angry because you are buying into the same *"whites accept you"* lie that Michael Jackson and OJ Simpson believed until their legal troubles reminded them that they are not white no matter how much money they had and how accepted they may have felt.

I'm angry because the same black folks these two celebrities looked down on and moved away from were the same ones who were in their corner when the verdict of not guilty was given, the same ones who embraced them after white society had rejected them. Why are we as a people so forgiving of our wayward snobs? Is it weakness or strength?

I'm still angry that I skulked out of a conference room because my all white coworkers were so angry and devastated with OJ's "not guilty" verdict. I was actually embarrassed by my secret pleasure that a black man got away with exposing the white legal system as the fraud it is: money will always trump justice. Wow, that was twenty years ago, but I remember it as though it were yesterday.

I'm angry because you, my son, are naïve. I'm angry that you actually believe there is a way you can act that will appease and make you invisible to haters and racist cops. You have never seen my anger at having to set an example about how to tiptoe in society so that you are not tagged a militant.

I'm angry because you feel invincible as far as becoming a Trayvon Martin or Walter Scott or an Emmett Till (Look that one up, son!).

I'm angry because you can't relate to these dead black men and boys—that you feel their history is not yours. I've tiptoed too well.

I'm angry because you told me you had been stopped by the police because your brake light was not working and that the cop actually had to teach you how to respond to police.

I'm angry that your dad didn't teach you that.

I'm angry because when I taught you to stay away from strangers, look both ways before crossing the street, and respect adults, I didn't know I also needed to teach you to not get out of the car to greet an approaching cop, but to have the sense to put your hands where he could see them and wait for his approach.

I'm angry because I shouldn't have to protect you from the police whose salaries my tax dollars go toward so that they will protect you.

Wait. I say I'm angry but am I really? Anger is exhausting. You are thirty-one years old now because God has kept you. Like countless black mothers before me from slavery to now, I have turned to God and the church to keep you protected. There was a time when the black church was the normal, respected route of protection for our black boys and men. I have prayerfully covered you with the blood of Jesus and prayed in the spirit for your protection—a black mother's weapon for centuries. I have trusted in the only proven shield for the lives of black men in this day and time—God.

So, my son, it's no longer a secret how I feel. As a pastor, I see you carrying the mantle that will help protect other black boys and men. Change is coming. The house slave and field slave mentality is a lie. When churched and unchurched black people realize that we're all in this together, real power for change can begin again. I have no more secrets and I'm glad.

You are a man now and can hear these final words on anger. I've heard it said that hypertension in blacks is hereditary. But I say that tiptoeing around in society is hereditary. You don't have to tiptoe when you speak to injustice. My wonderful, handsome, and strong son, make sure you don't hold onto anger.

31

A LETTER TO DR. KING

Please Keep Breathing

Maria del Guadalupe Davidson

Dear Dr. King:[1]

I hope this letter finds you well. My name is Maria del Guadalupe and although we have not met, I have known about you my entire life. When I was a little girl growing up in Syracuse, New York, in the 1970s, I remember that all black homes I visited had three pictures hanging on the wall: yours, John F. Kennedy's, and Jesus's! You are one of the first names I learned in school. Your words are some of the first that I ever committed to memory—like poems and promises. You and I are both Capricorns and we both earned PhDs. We both are completely committed to the social gospel. I even coauthored an article about you and the French philosopher Emmanuel Levinas where we (my husband and I) described you as a "post-Holocaust thinker" because your thinking is profoundly shaped by the holocaust of black enslavement. You have been a significant part of my entire life, both personal and academic. For these reasons, I feel confident that you will not mind me telling you about some things that have been weighting on *this mother's heart*.

Even in heaven, I'm sure that you are aware that young black people are not faring well in our society. Young black children (especially if they are poor) are being warehoused in schools that are not teaching them. Countless black people are unemployed or underemployed, and health disparities and income inequality have become woven into the very fabric of the black community. Black people, especially those living

in our inner cities, are doing very poorly. Since the death of Eric Garner, who was literally choked to death, many black people from all
walks of life have taken up Garner's last words—"I can't breathe"—as
an indictment against a society where black lives don't seem to matter;
as a call for justice when there is actual visual proof of police miscon-
duct; as a statement of fact when black people are as beautiful and as
valuable as anyone else and yet are socially and existentially suffocating
from racist ills; and, as prayer for relief from this pain.

Dr. King, this society is literally restricting black breath, squeezing
black folks so tight with its racism that at any moment it feels like
millions of black people may suffocate. When Eric Garner was murdered, I felt that there was nothing that I could say to uplift others
around me who were hurting just like me. For the very first time in my
life, I felt so drained, so low in energy. I had no words of wisdom,
nothing to make my pain, their pain, or anyone's pain, go away. I was,
like so many others, in a state of "walking wounded." When Eric Garner
died that was one of the critical moments in my life when I felt compelled to go to my knees in prayer, because there was nowhere else to
go. Yet, even then I was unsure about what to ask for. How many times
have black folk laid our burdens at the foot of the cross with the cry of
"help!" being the only word we were able to speak? In that moment,
what should I have prayed for? Do I pray for peace or justice or safety
for all the black boys and men, women and girls who walk every day into
streets where they are at risk? These are streets where their bodies lay
shot up, decaying in the hot sun, choked to death or are thrown in the
back of police cars when they try to express concern for a murdered
love one.

Do I pray for mothers and wives, sisters, and brothers who sit with
grace at the front of the church while their own souls lay dying deep
inside of them? As a black mother, I don't want to sit in the pew, with a
fan, wearing black and trying my damn best to look strong. What if
someone hurts one of my sons, Dr. King? I would lose my mind. Dr.
King, how far am I from that pew? Given this society, I shudder to even
ponder such a question. In reality, as a mother of black children, I know
I'm not that far from that pew. I can get that call, hear those sirens, and
then feel that grief. Dr. King, I'm tired of black men, boys, and people
dying. I'm tired of worrying about the safety of my sons, brothers,

cousins, and other family members. I'm tired of worrying about *all* black men and *all* black people.

Dr. King, I honestly believe that there is something horrible that happens when lives are lost so violently and so suddenly. I believe that when people are murdered, the very act causes dread and an unspeakable pain. This is why I truly believe that Eric, Trayvon, Tamir Rice, Michael Brown, Renisha McBride and countless other black souls are in pain and looking for peace. Their lives were taken from them, much like yours. I am not one to talk about death as we often do in our community, with an acceptance that "it was so and so's time to go." I tend to use the street language I grew up with to describe violent acts: "bullets have no names." Like bullets, the targets of white supremacy have no names. That is, when it comes to white supremacy, it does not matter who you are. You are at risk simply for being black. How do we seek peace to somehow ease the passing and pain of Trayvon, Tamir, Michael, Eric, Renisha, and countless others, how do we do this, Dr. King?

In search of an answer to my questions, I return to your words and encourage my friends to do so as well. There I do not only find a balm to heal broken hearts, but I find a blueprint for action. In your "Letter from Birmingham Jail," you talk about a similar type of fear to the one that I have been describing:

> As in so many past experiences, our hopes had been blasted, and the shadow of deep disappointment settled upon us. We had no alternative except to prepare for direct action, whereby we would present our very bodies as a means of laying our case before the conscience of the local and the national community.[2]

All over this country, people have participated in direct action; these are no longer called "sit-ins"; now they are called "die-ins." They are spectacular sights that prick the conscience of society. People are also protesting through the simple action of wearing tee shirts with the phrase "I can't breathe." People are putting their bodies in harm's way and stopping traffic to prove the point that black lives matter.

As you write:

> We know through painful experience that freedom is never voluntarily given by the oppressor; it must be demanded by the oppressed.

Frankly, I have yet to engage in a direct action campaign that was "well timed" in the view of those who have not suffered unduly from the disease of segregation. For years now I have heard the word "Wait!" It rings in the ear of every Negro with piercing familiarity. This "Wait" has almost always meant "Never." We must come to see, with one of our distinguished jurists, that "justice too long delayed is justice denied."[3]

It is a pity that those very same words that you wrote over sixty years ago are still so relevant today. Yet, I know that we can use your words and find strength and meaning in them. These tragic events (as well as the next event, because there is always a next one coming) will *NOT* break us. In spite of it all, I will never stop working for justice.

You know this is completely random, Dr. King, but the other day I was looking at all the magnets and pictures that hang on our refrigerator. Here's a snapshot of what is there:

- "Bring me a bowl of coffee before I turn into a goat."—Johann Sebastian Bach
- "Be gentle with yourself. You are a child of the universe, no less than the trees and the stars. In the noisy confusion of life, keep peace in your soul."—Max Ehrmann
- "Never, Never, Never Give Up."—Winston Churchill

Of all the random things hanging on my fridge, this is my favorite one:

- "We will meet all of us women [and men] of every land. We will meet in the center, make a circle. We will weave a world web to entangle the powers that bury our children." [4]

I often think about these words and how to put them into action. But, in writing to you, I have arrived at some new ideas of my own. First of all, it begins with naming the names of those powers that bury our children, including, but not limited to: lack of opportunity, poverty, inequality, racial profiling, hetero-normativity, and all of the -isms. These must be named as enemies of life, liberty, and the pursuit of happiness. We must work to entangle these powers so that we can protect our children. Dr. King, before I end my letter here, I'd like to share with you the words of our first African American president, Mr. Barack Hussein Obama:

> We, the people, declare today that the most evident of truths—that all of us are created equal—is the star that guides us still; just as it guided our forebears through Seneca Falls and Selma and Stonewall; just as it guided all those men and women, sung and unsung, who left footprints along this great Mall, to hear a preacher say that we cannot walk alone; to hear a King proclaim that our individual freedom is inextricably bound to the freedom of every soul on earth. [5]

"Our individual freedom is inextricably bound to the freedom of every soul on earth." [6] This simple truth could save countless black and brown lives. I thank you for your patience, Dr. King. If you see my mom in heaven, please tell her that I miss her.

Lupe

32

A LETTER TO MY SONS

Dawn Herd-Clark

Dear Deondri and Donyae:

To my two beloved sons, I am writing this letter to you to let you know that you are more than the fifteen-to-thirty-second negative segments of death that you see on television. I want you to know that you both originate from African kings, and that you are royalty in the eyes of your family. I pray that you do not suffer the fate of males of African descent including Trayvon Martin, Dontre Hamilton, Eric Garner, John Crawford III, Michael Brown Jr., Ezell Ford, Dante Parker, Akai Gurley, Tamir Rice, Eric Harris, Walter Scott, and Freddie Gray. I want you to know that your life *DOES* matter and that I will do all that I can to help you to instill pride in your heritage. I pray that you both have an opportunity to grow up and become intelligent, caring, outstanding pillars in our community.

One of your ancestors is King Tutankhamun, who is more commonly known as King Tut. Only nine years old when he ascended to the throne, the same age as you, Donyae, the boy emperor ruled Egypt from 1332 BCE until 1323 BCE; and Egypt is on the African continent. Although young in age when he became Egypt's ruler, King Tut is noted in history for helping the empire improve its relationship with neighboring empires, and documentation indicates that he was good at archery, something I know that you, Deondri, want to try. King Tut virtually disappeared from history until his tomb was discovered in 1922. Upon its opening, priceless artifacts from his life were found well preserved, including jewelry, artwork, and perfumes.

Another great emperor on the continent of Africa prior to European contact was Mansa Musa, known as the richest man in history; he ruled the Mali Empire from 1312 to 1337. The wealth of Mansa Musa was documented when the leader made his Hajj to Mecca. Mansa Musa's entourage included thousands of people and gifts of gold, which he distributed along the way. I see Mansa Musa's spirit of giving in you both; Deondri and Donyae, you are willing to assist those in need whenever called upon. Mansa Musa also strengthened education in his kingdom upon his return by building libraries and universities for his people. Deondri and Donyae, the two of you followed in the tradition set by Mansa Musa when you both made the A Honor Roll this year!

As the age of exploration began, during the 1400s, people of African descent appeared in the Americas. Popular television will tell you that Africans first came to America enslaved, but not all were. One such noted person is believed to have been Jean Baptiste Point du Sable; the first settler of Chicago. Sources indicate that this Haitian immigrant initially served as a fur trader in Indiana. Du Sable then moved to the Chicago area where he and his family became prosperous farmers known throughout the young nation. I know that you both, Deondri and Donyae, want to visit Chicago, but it is important for you to know that a man of African descent helped lay the foundation for the great city that it is today.

Although all Africans were not brought to America for enslavement, the "peculiar institution" existed in all thirteen colonies. Despite the fact that most Africans were enslaved, they were NOT stripped of their culture, and they made notable contributions. One aspect of African culture that they brought with them that is still evident in the African American community is the importance of music. Music is an ancient art form on the continent of Africa and it influenced all aspects of their lives, including the birth of a child, religious ceremonies, war, and even death. Such a concept of music was brought to the thirteen original British mainland colonies, and the enslaved people used it in their clandestine religious services and when they worked in the field harvesting crops. I see that same musical tradition in both of you. Deondri, you play percussion in the Fort Valley Middle School band, and Donyae, you are always singing a melody or dropping sixteen bars.

As the colonies in the new world developed, a labor source was needed. Although Africans were not the first laborers used, enslaved

Africans became the most permanent form of forced workers for the colonies. Despite having been enslaved, people of African descent played a role in the British mainland colonies. They helped the colonists to secure their independence from the British Empire. People of African descent could easily relate to the ideas of "freedom" and "liberty" expressed by colonists. One such person of African descent who fought gallantly for the American revolutionary cause was Salem Poor; his commanders stated that he "behaved like an experienced officer as well as an excellent soldier."[1] Deondri and Donyae, you both behave gallantly as young men of African descent like your ancestor, Salem Poor.

The American Revolution proved to be a contradiction for the United States. Despite the fact that the Constitution was written declaring that "all men are created equal," racial and gender oppression continued. One free person of African descent who emerged during this era was Benjamin Banneker, who is noted in history for his contributions to astronomy and math. Mostly self-educated, Banneker not only helped survey Washington D.C., but he also wrote annual almanacs which included segments on astronomical calculations, literature, and political commentary. I want you both to know, Deondri and Donyae, that I see the same intellectual curiosity that drove Benjamin Banneker to achieve such greatness in you.

Although the institution of slavery was phased out in the northern states after the American Revolution, it spread throughout the South due to a new profitable cash crop, cotton. While most people of African descent were enslaved in the South, they did not allow their circumstance to determine their ability. One prominent individual who changed his circumstances was noted abolitionist and orator Frederick Douglass. Born enslaved, Douglass lived with various "masters." It was at the Auld household where Douglass was exposed to education; Sophia Auld taught him the alphabet. That educational foundation impassioned Douglass to continue to educate himself and other enslaved Africans that he encountered. To punish Douglass for his "rebellious" spirit, he was sent to Edward Covey, a noted "slave breaker." Despite the beatings that he endured, Douglass knew that his lot in life was to be free, which led to his successful escape from the brutal institution in 1838. Not satisfied with his freedom solely, Douglass became the most famous abolitionist in terms of his oratory and numerous lectures; and his written legacy includes various autobiographies, including *Narrative of the Life of Frederick Douglass, An American Slave*, and *My Bondage and My Freedom*; and his newspapers, including *The North Star, Frederick Douglass Weekly*, and the *New National Era*. Deondri and Donyae, as you both advance in life, I don't want you to be satisfied with your own circumstances solely, but you must help uplift others.

The legal enslavement of people of African descent in the United States ended after the Civil War with the passage of the Thirteenth Amendment, in 1865. During Reconstruction, two other significant amendments were added to the United States Constitution, the Fourteenth Amendment, in 1868, which extended citizenship to people of African descent, and the Fifteenth Amendment, in 1870, which granted the franchise to Black men. It was during this era that many politicians of African descent emerged on the scene. One such noted politician was Hiram R. Revels, from Fayetteville, North Carolina, where you, Donyae, were born. Revels became the first African American United States senator; he represented the citizens of Mississippi, filling the seat that Jefferson Davis once held. A barber and minister, Revels fought for the Union during the Civil War, and saw action at the Battle of Vicksburg. After the war ceased, Revels moved to Mississippi where his political career began. Revels spent his later years preaching, and became president of Alcorn Agricultural and Mechanical College. Deondri and Donyae, I want you both to keep education and faith as key foundational elements in your life.

According to William Edward Burghardt Du Bois, noted scholar and activist, in 1903, "the problem of the Twentieth Century is the problem of the color line."[2] As a child, Du Bois attended integrated schools in Massachusetts. However, it was his collegiate years at Fisk University that brought the issue of racism most powerfully to the forefront of his consciousness. Du Bois went on to make his mark in American history by becoming the first person of African descent to earn a doctorate from Harvard University, eventually writing the first case study of an African American community, *The Philadelphia Negro: A Social Study*, and cofounding the National Association for the Advancement of Colored People and founding its official publication, *The Crisis*. Early in his career, Du Bois embraced Pan-Africanism, the idea that people of African descent should work together worldwide. Deondri and Donyae, as you progress in life, remember to be like Du Bois, remember to nurture your intellectual ambitions and to help people of African descent around the world.

Despite the circumstances that African Americans were facing, culturally they continued to thrive, which culminated in the 1920s and 1930s in Harlem, New York. The Harlem Renaissance, also known as the New Negro Movement, was the first time that African American culture, which included music, art, and literature, was appreciated by the larger American public. One outstanding contributor to this movement was Paul Robeson. Robeson, the world-renowned singer and actor, began as a noted student athlete while in college. The Rutgers University standout earned over ten letters in four varsity sports while a member of Phi Beta Kappa and valedictorian of his class. Robeson furthered his education by attending law school, but turned to acting due to racism at the law firm that employed him. Robeson initially starred in Broadway productions, but his outstanding reputation led him to acting bookings in Europe, making him an international sensation. Robeson became known for his acting abilities, both on the stage and big screen, and singing repertoire, including spirituals, classical music, and world folk songs. However, his greatest contribution to mankind was his Civil Rights activities. Robeson utilized his fame to help liberate oppressed peoples around the world, from America to South Africa. Even when it destroyed his entertainment career, Robeson refused to remain silent. Deondri and Donyae, I want you both to show the courage of Paul Robeson when facing adversity because you are willing to speak "the truth."

While the men of African descent above laid the general foundation for you both, the African American men who have played the most important role in your formative years thus far include your maternal grandfather, Walter Henry Herd, your paternal grandfather, David Lee Clark, and your father, Deondri Lendrake Clark. Herd made history as one of the first African Americans to enter the University of Missouri in 1955. Despite very difficult periods of racism and discrimination, Herd, a mechanical engineering graduate, worked for the United States Army Corps of Engineers for over twenty-five years to support his family. David Clark is noted in history for working hard and supporting his family. The migrant farmer garnered the reputation for picking the most oranges the quickest. And despite the fact that his job required him to move throughout the country due to the various harvest seasons, he always put his family first. Deondri Clark is noted for being the first African American former Florida State University football player to become a collegiate head football coach, and he spends his time teaching young men how to use their athletic abilities to fund their education. Deondri and Donyae, you are BLESSED to have these three key men in your life; they are all outstanding examples of African American men.

Deondri and Donyae, I leave you both the legacy of your forefathers; they were political leaders, explorers, soldiers, Civil Rights activists, scholars, actors, engineers, migrant farmers, and coaches. With this knowledge, I want to empower you both to achieve all your goals. Trayvon Martin, Dontre Hamilton, Eric Garner, John Crawford III, Michael Brown Jr., Ezell Ford, Dante Parker, Akai Gurley, Tamir Rice, Eric Harris, Walter Scott, and Freddie Gray all had the same historical lineage that I've painted above. Yet, their lives were taken away by those who were and are empowered by their communities to protect and/or serve them. Deondri and Donyae, I want and encourage you to use this rich legacy to educate others to help sustain and strengthen the community that we, as Black people and people of color, live in.

With all my love,

Mommy

AFTERWORD

Farah Jasmine Griffin

In Memory of Willie B. Hendricks, mother of Obery M. Hendricks

I am not a mother. I have loved many black boys; I have never given birth to or raised one. Therefore I read each of these eloquent statements about mothering black sons with a sense of curiosity, admiration, and wonder. The voices within these pages belong to diverse women. They cross lines of race, nationality, and religion. However, they are united in these ways: They love their sons with a primal fierceness and a sweet tenderness. They live in awe of what stands before them and with a constant sense of fear. They confront the absurd paradox that America desires, distrusts, and disdains black men; this nation is fascinated with and fearful of black men. And it all starts in boyhood. Finally each is riddled by a series of questions. How do you raise a black boy to be a man, to have a true sense of himself, made in the image of God, while still ensuring his safety? How do you raise him to be fearless but not naïve to the forces arrayed against them? These women are vigilant, even in their sleep.

There are hauntings and echoes within these pages. From autobiographical narrative and analytical essay to poetry and the epistolary form, we see women grappling with the legacy of black motherhood. The litany of names that appear and reappear—Emmett, Trayvon, Mike, Tamir—is a constant reminder of the fate that haunts the lives of black boys, black children. The knowledge that all the care in the world may not protect them from death is countered only by the power of black art—music, poetry, and painting—to teach, to represent, to shape, and to give grounding to a growing spirit. These women teach black boys to stand tall in traditions that will nurture and sustain them. Together, the collection as a whole echoes another multi-generic text, *The Souls of Black Folk*. It may be one of many responses to the call issued by that founding text. And just as DuBois brought every critical and creative tool to bear upon his description and analysis of black life, so too do the writers here. Recall that Dr. DuBois also turned to elegy, poetry, and song. Recall "On the Passing of the First Born," his meditation on the death of his own golden boy. Perhaps it is the deep resonance with *Souls* that makes Noliwe Rooks's sentence so painfully insightful. "We knew that guns were not the only way to murder a Black male soul."

And yet, there runs through these pages a sense of hope. For each of these writers insists upon black life. In the very act of giving birth, the very act of bearing witness, the very act of devoting oneself to black children, is an act of faith and a commitment to changing the world. For it seems that knowing and loving black sons transforms the mother by making her more aware, making her imagine what it is to live in a body so unlike her own. If you are a white mother of a black son, your love for him can transform your own relationship to whiteness. If you are a black mother of a black son, your love of him grounds you, blood bone deep, in a history that is both terrifying and beautiful. No matter what, that love seems to strip you of any remaining innocence.

In reading these eloquent, brilliant pieces, I also found myself thinking of the mothers who are not fully here, though thankfully their voices are represented in the essays: the mothers who live with the reality of being not only black, but also poor; the ones whose eloquence may be of tongue and not pen. And I know, they are no less afraid, in fact, they may be more so: They fear police, racist vigilantes, and all too often young men who look like their sons. They fear poverty and the temptations of doubt and despair. They too are among the courageous ones. To be courageous and hopeful is not to be without fear. It is to insist on life in the face of death, it is to keep going in spite of fear; it is to walk through the fire, not above or beyond it.

There is a beautiful Christmas song, written by Mark Lowry and Buddy Green, "Mary Did You Know." Whenever I hear it I am so moved by the lyrics, addressed to the mother of Christ, herself a teenage mother, who loved a gifted and courageous son only to watch him die at the hands of empire. That story, which has become sacrilized, that image of the Pieta, of the Mother holding her dead son's body, so resonates with the history of black mothers and sons. The song poses questions to Mary that I pose to mothers of black sons: What do you think at their birth? Did you look at their limbs, count their fingers, trace the curve of their mouths? Did you have a moment to think of their futures without the veil and shadow of fear that is sure to come? Did you know even then that this perfect child would require your love, your protection, and your constant prayer? That this child, born to be a man, a father, a leader, a worker, a star, would have to live in a world that did not always welcome him? Did you know? You raise him and keep him, as best you can, from the soul murder, gunfire at the hands of peers or police. Even if he becomes president of the United States (you never had any doubt he would), your fear only increases. The threat to his life is only made stronger by the level of his achievement, visibility, and exercise of power. Did you know? And, if he dares to be a freedom-loving, justice-seeking man, a Martin, Malcolm, Medgar, like Christ himself, . . . well . . .

These women know. All too well.

Much within these pages is written by women who gave birth to black boys; others are by women who reared and nurtured them. Then there are those who have observed and studied the cost, consequences, and joy of having done so. To read their words is to know what it means to love profoundly and hopefully we come away committed to a world where the mother of a black boy does not have to live in fear of the inevitability that someone will try to do him physical or psychic harm. We leave this remarkable collection knowing that loving black sons is transformative and transforming, knowing that mothers of black sons are women of vision and agents of change.

NOTES

INTRODUCTION

1. http://opinionator.blogs.nytimes.com/2013/09/01/walking-while-black-in-the-white-gaze/?_r=0 (accessed March 8, 2016).

2. Khalil Gibran Muhammad, *The Condemnation of Blackness: Race, Crime, and the Meaning of Modern Urban America* (Cambridge, MA: Harvard University Press, 2010), 21.

3. Frantz Fanon, *Black Skin, White Masks*, trans. Charles Lam Markman (New York: Grove Press, 1967), 139; first published in 1952.

4. Patricia J. Williams, *Seeing a Color-Blind Future: The Paradox of Race* (New York: Farrar, Straus and Giroux, 1997), 15.

5. Williams, *Seeing a Color-Blind Future*, 15.

6. Cornel West, *Brother West: Living and Loving Out Loud, A Memoir* (New York: Smiley Books, 2010), 27.

7. West, *Brother West*, 29.

8. Patricia J. Williams, *The Rooster's Egg: On the Persistence of Prejudice* (Cambridge, MA: Harvard University Press, 1995), 185.

9. For an importantly engaging treatment of the political, historical, and philosophical tragic death of Trayvon Martin, see George Yancy and Janine Jones, eds. *Pursuing Trayvon Martin: Historical Contexts and Contemporary Manifestations of Racial Dynamics* (Lanham, MD: Lexington Books, 2013).

1. BLACK MOTHER/SONS

1. W. E. B. Du Bois, *The Souls of Black Folk* (New York: The New American Library, 1982), 45.

2. Michelle Alexander, *The New Jim Crow: Mass Incarceration in the Age of Colorblindness* (New York: The New Press, 2012).

2. ONCE WHITE IN AMERICA

1. *Strange Fruit,* lyrics from poem by Lewis Allen.

2. The story referred to in this essay is "Fictions of Home," originally published as a chapter in the novel, *Worlds Beyond My Control* (New York: Dutton, 1991) and anthologized in Donna Bassin, Margaret Honey, and Meryle Mahrer Kaplan, *Representations of Motherhood* (New Haven, CT: Yale University Press, 1994).

3. 1863—Date of Emancipation Proclamation.

4. 1968—Date of the Voting Rights Act.

5. 2008—Date of the election of Barack Obama as president of the United States.

4. DARK RADIANCE

1. Afaa Michael Weaver, "Remember" (for his granddaughter), in *The Government of Nature* (Pittsburgh: University of Pittsburgh, 2013), 36.

2. Manning Marable, *How Capitalism Underdeveloped Black America* (Boston: South End, 1983), 118.

3. Jennifer Gonnerman, "Brutal Territory," review of *Ghettoside: A True Story of Murder in America, New York Times Book Review*, January 25, 2015, 20.

11. BLACK AND BLUE

1. https://www.whitehouse.gov/the-press-office/2013/07/19/remarks-president-trayvon-martin (accessed May 15, 2015).

2. http://salsa.net/peace/conv/8weekconv6-4.html (accessed May 15, 2015).

13. SACRIFICIAL LAMBS

1. John Edgar Wideman, "The Killing of Black Boys," *Essence*, November 1997, http://www.emmetttillmurder.com/Wideman.htm (accessed April 18, 2015).

2. Ishmael Reed, *Writing Is Fightin': Thirty-Seven Years of Boxing on Paper* (New York: Atheneum Books, 1988).

3. Reed, *Writing Is Fightin'*.

4. Nelson Mandela, *Long Walk to Freedom: Autobiography of Nelson Mandela* (New York: Back Bay Books, 1995), 391.

5. Audre Lorde, *Sister Outsider: Essays and Speeches* (Berkeley, CA: Crossing Press, 2007). Reprint, 41.

14. REFLECTIONS OF BLACK MOTHERHOOD

1. Frederick Douglass, "Address to the Louisville Convention," September 24, 1883, http://www.anselm.edu/academic/history/hdubrulle/civwar/text/documents/doc55.htm (accessed June 1, 2015).

2. Ecclesiastes 9:3, King James Bible; Stephen Hawking, *People Daily Online*, June 14, 2006, https://en.wikiquote.org/wiki/Stephen_Hawking (accessed June 1, 2015).

15. THE WAR WITHIN

1. M. Maltais. (2014). "Raising a Black Son," *Los Angles Times*, http://www.latimes.com/opinion/opinion-la/la-ol-raising-black-brown-boys-ferguson-20140815-story.html (accessed January 27, 2015).

2. M. Smith. (2014). "Affect and Respectability Politics," *Theory and Event*, 17(3), https://muse.jhu.edu/article/559376 (accessed January 23, 2015).

3. S. J. Pope. (1999). "The Moral Primacy of Basic Respect," *Cross Currents* 49(1): 54–62.

4. I am cognizant of the fact that mothers of Black children are not always Black, and individuals who raise Black sons are not always racially Black or females. For example, there are white mothers, both natural and adoptive, and gay men raising Black sons.

5. A. Crittenden. "The Price of Motherhood: Why the Most Important Job in the World Is Still the Least Valued," in *Women, Images, and Realities: A*

Multicultural Anthology, 5th edition, edited by S. G. Kelly (New York: McGraw Hill, 2012), 88–91.

6. J. B. Comey. (n.d.). "Hard Truths, Law Enforcement, and Race," FBI.gov, http://www.fbi.gov/news/speeches/hard-truths-law-enforcement-and-race (accessed February 18, 2015).

7. L. Miller. (2014). "Racialized State Failure and the Violent Death of Michael Brown," *Theory and Event* 17(3 Supplement), https://muse.jhu.edu/article/559374, accessed 23, 2015.

8. Lionel C. Howard, Jason C. Rose, and Oscar A. Barbarin. (2013). "Raising African American Boys: An Exploration of Gender and Racial Socialization Practices," *American Journal of Orthopsychiatry* 83(2.3), 218–230. doi:10 1111ajop 12031.

9. Howard, Rose, and Barbarin, "Raising African American Boys," 228.

10. B. Brandon-Croft. (July 30, 2013). "Raising a Black Boy in America," *Parents*, http://www.parents.com/blogs/parents-perspective/2013/07/30/news/raising-a-black-boy-in-america/ (accessed January 27, 2015).

11. Many of us, mothers of Black sons, can identify with Brandon-Croft's maternal angst that engenders race-based socialization messages (lectures) to her son, such as the following:

> He'll have to be told that in another six or seven years, that he's not only likely to be a victim, but will also be seen, in the eyes of many, as an [*sic*] suspect—for nothing other than the color of his skin. That hanging out with one or more of his black friends outside will turn "the guys" into "a gang" and, depending on who's [looking] at them, "a threat"—and it won't matter if they're carrying basketballs and water bottles. My son will have to be taught that he can't be "mischievous" like his white counterparts are allowed to be. Carrying out a dare to steal a candy bar for a white friend might garner him a "time out," and that same misdeed could get my son shot. A teenager's "joy ride" is just that for a white boy, but translates to grand larceny for my son. As bleak as it may sound, he has to be taught— for safety sake—that racism exists.
>
> I had to give the Trayvon talk to my son and his friend as they headed out to the park last night. (A lecture that, I'm sure, echoes the one Emmett Till's mom gave her son before she sent him down south that summer.) I told my son and his friend that if they are approached by anyone of "authority" (fake cops included) that they had to be ultra-polite ("Yes, sirs." and "Yes, ma'ams"). I explained that they were to answer any questions directed to them clearly and with-

out sarcasm (which is precisely what, at their age, they are develop-
mentally hard-wired to do). And I told them that although it may not
be fair, I would rather have them humbled than harmed . . . or
worse. (Brandon-Croft, 2013)

Similar sentiments are expressed by Christopher Thangaraj in the following:

My husband and I dread the day we'll have to tell our teenage sons
that the world will not treat them like their white peers. In any
confrontations with the police, we will advise them to be polite to the
point of being obsequious and always insist the police call us immediately. Their youthful indiscretions will make them accountable as
adults and they will be judged on a different and unfair standard. It is
unfair, it is unjust and it is maddening. But it is reality. How can we
ask them to understand something we ourselves don't?
(http://www.huffingtonpost.com/christopher-thangaraj/the-reality-
of-raising-african-american-boys-in-america_b_5712299.html)

12. Prominently positioned in recent social advocacy against police brutality
are mothers of Black men who are killed by law enforcement officers, real and
fake. For example, CODEPINK, a transnational feminist activist network,
foregrounds mothers of slain Black men in advocating for law enforcement
reforms that would address police brutality. http://www.codepink.org/grieving_
mothers_come_to_washington_dc. Mothers against Police Brutality is another
grassroots activist group that highlights the plight of mothers of slain sons.
http://www.mothersagainstpolicebrutality.com/.

16. A LONG WAYS FROM HOME?

1. The medley was originally released in 1956 as part of an album entitled
Bless This House. It was reissued in the early 1960s in an album entitled *The
Best of Mahalia Jackson*, Vol. 2. A video clip of a television broadcast of Jackson
performing the song, excerpted from a 1958 television special starring Bing
Crosby, is available online at https://www.youtube.com/watch?v=
hohnr22zTxcis.
2. An especially helpful account of the relationship between the two songs
is offered by Samuel A. Floyd in *The Power of Black Music: Interpreting Its
History from Africa to the United States* (Oxford: Oxford University Press,

1997), 218–20. See also Howard Pollack, *George Gershwin: His Life and Work* (Berkeley and Los Angeles: University of California Press, 2007), 662.

3. Michelle Alexander offers a compelling account of the problematic evolution of late-twentieth-century American law in her book *The New Jim Crow: Mass Incarceration in the Age of Colorblindness*, revised edition (New York: The New Press, 2012).

4. There is considerable controversy about the numbers of such killings that actually occur, and an equally potent controversy about whether such killings are justified. But a study by the public-interest journalist organization ProPublica has shown, for instance, that African American males are twenty-one times more likely than their white peers to be killed by police. See the full report at http://www.propublica.org/article/deadly-force-in-black-and-white. A useful account of the meaning of these statistics is provided by Brent Staples at http://takingnote.blogs.nytimes.com/2014/10/10/whos-killing-all-those-black-men-and-boys/.

5. For a discussion of this habit of constructing Black males as "permanent possibilities of danger," see Moody-Adams, "Race, Class and The Social Construction of Self-Respect," *Philosophical Forum* 24(1–3) (Fall–Spring 1993), 251–66.

6. I made a similar argument in 1991, not long after the start of the hip-hop revolution in http://www.nytimes.com/1990/06/25/opinion/l-don-t-confuse-2-live-crew-with-black-culture-957290.html.

7. James Baldwin, "Notes of a Native Son," in James Baldwin, *Collected Essays* (New York: Library of America, 1998), 87.

17. T.H.U.G. (TALENTED, HUMANISTIC, UNIQUE, GIFTED)

1. Renato Rosado, "Introduction: Grief and a Headhunter's Rage," in *Culture and Truth: The Remaking of Social Analysis* (Boston and London: Beacon Press and Taylor and Francis, 1993 and 1989), 25.

2. Raymond Williams, "Structures of Feeling" in *Marxism and Literature* (Oxford: Oxford University Press, 1977), 130.

3. Michel Foucault, "Nietzsche, Genealogy, History." In *Language, Counter-Memory, Practice: Selected Essays and Interviews*, edited by D. F. Bouchard (Ithaca: Cornell University Press, 1977), 80.

4. Foucault, "Nietzsche, Genealogy, History," 81.

5. "Interview: Alice Walker." *Foreign Policy*, June 23, 2011.

6. Roxane Gay, "What We Hunger For," 2012, https://therumpus.net/2012/04/what-we-hunger-for.

7. Norbert Elias, *The Civilizing Process: Sociogenetic and Psychogenetic Investigations* (Oxford: Blackwell Publishers, 1994 [1939]), 230.

18. A FIERCE LOVE

1. William H. Frey, "New Projections Point to a Majority Minority Nation in 2044," *Brookings Institute* (December 12, 2014), http://www.brookings.edu/blogs/the-avenue/posts/2014/12/12-majority-minority-nation-2044-frey (accessed February 4, 2015).

2. Bonnie Berman Cushing, "White Fear of Black Men," *Center for the Study of White American Culture* (March 10, 2013), http://euroamerican.org/wordpress/index.php/2013/03/10/white-fear-of-black-men/ (accessed January 11, 2015). "As a nation we seem to have very short memories. Fear of the Black man just didn't start overnight, and it didn't just happen during the course of our lifetime; like any singularity it has to have a beginning. Its origin has been embedded in this nation's consciousness since the Nat Turner revolt; a pathological fear that the oppressed will one day rise up and inflict vengeance upon the oppressor." Citing M. Gibson, comments on a blog related to the shooting of Black male Oscar Grant by a police officer in Oakland, California.

3. "Psychologists call them transitional objects, but your baby may call hers 'Bankie' (for blanket). Many doctors say bonding with a 'lovey,' a special blanket or toy, can ease a child's adjustment to new situations such as daycare." See, "Does Your Baby Have a Lovey?" Baby Center, http://www.babycenter.com/4_does-your-baby-have-a-lovey_4587.bc (accessed January 11, 2015).

4. When my son was an infant, we established a routine for naptime and bedtime that allowed for routinely peaceful transitions. When I instructed my son that it was time to take a nap or go to bed for the evening, I took him to his room, tucked him in his bed, and read him a story before he went to sleep. There were also infrequent occasions when he would take the initiative to tell me that he was taking a nap without the need of me putting him in the bed or reading him a story.

5. Aggression is a label that has been applied to boys in schools as a means of punishment and control of behavior and interactions that one does not understand. See, Professor Joseph Tobin, PhD, "Understanding Boy Aggression," *Understanding and Raising Boys*, PBS Parents, http://www.pbs.org/parents/raisingboys/aggression02.html (accessed January 11, 2015).

6. As the mother of an African American child (male or female), one must mother with a light that transcends the darkness of racism and oppression that are present in our society today. Stephanie Buckhanon Crowder noted that "[a]s an African American mother of two sons living in the South, I find wom-

anist maternal thought fitting because there are unique racial, gender, economic, and religious conundrums that contribute to the complexity of what we
mothers do." Stephanie Buckhanon Crowder, "It's Complicated: Thoughts on
Nurturing African American Males," *Journal of Feminist Studies in Religion*
27(2) (Fall 2011), 137. V. Lawson Bush, "How Black Mothers Participate in the
Development of Manhood and Masculinity: What Do We Know about Black
Mothers and Their Sons?" *The Journal of Negro Education* 73(4) (Autumn,
2004), 381–91.

7. Colorism has been associated as an issue with females. However, males
are also affected by stereotypical issues related to masculinity and discipline.
Erica Williams Simon, "5 Things You Need to Know about Colorism," *Ebony*
(April 21, 2014), http://www.ebony.com/news-views/5-things-you-need-to-
know-about-colorism-784#axzz3QXwG8ZCA (accessed February 1, 2015).

8. *Black's Law Dictionary* (1990), 1447.

9. Josh Harkinson. "4 Unarmed Black Men Have Been Killed by Police in
the Last Month," *Mother Jones* (August 13, 2014, 8:50 p.m.), http://www.
motherjones.com/print/258296 (accessed February 4, 2015).

10. For approximately seven minutes after Eric Garner was released from a
chokehold from an NYPD officer, he lay on the sidewalk surrounded by approximately eight to ten police officers, and not one offered any medical assistance to an obviously unresponsive Garner. EMS finally arrived and trans-
ported Mr. Garner to the hospital where he was pronounced dead from cardiac
arrest. Emily Badger. "There Is a Second Eric Garner Video. It May Be More
Disturbing Than the First," *Washington Post* (December 5, 2014), http://www.
washingtonpost.com/blogs/wonkblog/wp/2014/12/05/there-is-a-second-eric-
garner-video-it-may-be-more-disturbing-than-the-first/ (accessed February 4,
2015).

11. "Timeline: Eric Garner Death," *4 New York*, NBC Affiliate (December
5, 2014, 9:44 a.m.), http://www.nbcnewyork.com/news/local/Timeline-Eric-
Garner-Chokehold-Death-Arrest-NYPD-Grand-Jury-No-Indictment-
284657081.html (accessed February 4, 2015).

12. The 9-1-1 caller, Ronald Ritchie, who reported that Mr. Crawford was
"waving a gun around and aiming at people, including two children" changed
his story after surveillance video from Walmart was released. The video shows
Mr. Crawford walking around the store with the air rifle at his side, occasional-
ly holding it up in the air, but not aiming it at any people. Jon Swain, "'It Was a
Crank Call' Family Seeks Action against 911 Caller in Walmart Shooting," *The
Guardian* (September 26, 2014, 4:02 p.m.), http://www.theguardian.com/
world/2014/sep/26/walmart-ohio-shooting-charges-911-calller-john-crawford
(accessed February 4, 2015).

13. "Hear the 911 Call about Tamir Rice: Gun Is 'Probably Fake' Caller Says," *LA Times* (November 26, 2014, 5:59 p.m.), http://www.latimes.com/nation/nationnow/la-na-nn-tamir-rice-911-call-20141126-htmlstory.html (accessed February 4, 2015).

14. "Tamir Rice: Police Release Video of 12-Year-Old's Fatal Shooting," *The Guardian* (November 26, 2014, 6:07 p.m.), http://www.theguardian.com/us-news/video/2014/nov/26/cleveland-video-tamir-rice-shooting-police (accessed February 4, 2015).

15. The presumption of innocence is defined as, "a hallowed principle of criminal law to the effect that the government has the burden of proving every element of a crime beyond a reasonable doubt and that the defendant has no burden to prove his innocence." *Black's Law Dictionary* (1990), 1186.

16. Social media Twitter tag #CrimingWhileWhite is a popular site for whites to post their encounters with the police to highlight the lenient punishment, if any, received for a crime that would have resulted in harsher punishment for Blacks. Reihan Salam, "What White Privilege Really Means," *Slate* (December 17, 2014, 12:22 a.m.), http://www.slate.com/articles/news_and_politics/politics/2014/12/criming_while_white_the_problem_with_our_conversation_about_white_privilege.html (accessed February 5, 2015).

17. Officer Darren Wilson provided grand jury testimony about his encounter with Michael Brown. He noted that Brown, "had the most intense, aggressive face. The only way I can describe it, it looks like a *demon*, that's how angry he looked." Amy Davidson, "Darren Wilson's Demon," *The New Yorker* (November 26, 2014), http://www.newyorker.com/news/amy-davidson/demon-ferguson-darren-wilson-fear-black-man (accessed February 5, 2015).

18. Tamir Rice was shot by the police within two seconds of their arriving on the scene, however, the video shows that the officers failed to render any medical attention to this child as he lay bleeding on the ground. Instead, the officers were concerned with handcuffing his fourteen-year-old sister who ran to the scene to check on her brother. "Cleveland Police Handcuff Tamir Rice's Sister after Shooting of 12-year-old," *The Guardian* (January 8, 2015, 4:36 p.m.), http://www.theguardian.com/us-news/video/2015/jan/08/new-video-tamir-rice-shooting-sister-video (accessed February 5, 2015). Tamir died at the hospital the following day as a result of his injuries from the gunshot wounds. "Tamir Rice: Police Release Video of 12-Year-Old's Fatal Shooting." *The Guardian.* It is a reasonable assumption to believe that his death may have been averted had immediate and appropriate medical attention been rendered at the scene. A lifeless Eric Garner lay on the ground for approximately seven minutes after being released from a chokehold, during which he told the officers numerous times "I can't breathe." No medical assistance was provided until EMS arrived. Emily Badger, "There Is a Second Eric Garner Video. It

May Be More Disturbing Than the First." These examples illustrate the stark disregard for the lives of Black males, their well-being, and their physical bodies. Most disturbing is the treatment of Michael Brown after his death. His body lay uncovered for four hours under the scorching August sun in the middle of Canfield Street, where he fell to the ground after being shot. Julie Bosman and Joseph Goldstein, "Timeline for a Body: 4 Hours in the Middle of a Ferguson Street," *New York Times* (August 23, 2014), http://www.nytimes. com/2014/08/24/us/michael-brown-a-bodys-timeline-4-hours-on-a-ferguson-street.html?_r=0 (accessed February 5, 2015). This act epitomizes a lack of respect and value for the body of a Black man, the pain felt by his family and the community.

19. The Young Men's Conference was held in Pittsburgh, Pennsylvania, at the Point Park University Campus on November 21, 2014. The Adonai Center's mission is "to support and promote the social, educational, and economic advancement of black males through human capital development. Our vision is to build a pipeline of leaders, innovators, and scholars who are valued as full and equal partners in our nation's progression." The Adonai Center for Black Males, http://www.adonaicenter.org/.

19. THROUGH THE VALLEY OF THE SHADOW OF DEATH

1. Elijah Cummings (Rep.), *Face the Nation.* Interview by Bob Schieffer, CBS, January 4, 2015.

2. Laura Van Dernoot Lipsky with Connie Burk, *Trauma Stewardship: An Everyday Guide to Caring for Self While Caring for Others* (San Francisco: Berrett-Koehler, 2009), 64.

3. Veronica T. Watson and Becky Thompson, "Theorizing White Racial Trauma and Its Remedies," in *Unveiling Whiteness in the Twenty-First Century: Global Manifestations, Transdisciplinary Interventions*, edited by Veronica Watson, Deirdre Howard-Wagner, and Lisa Spanierman (Lanham, MD: Lexington Books, 2014), 247–66: quote on page 250.

20. MOTHERS AND THEIR BLACK SONS

1. Langston Hughes, *Selected Poems of Langston Hughes* (New York: Vintage Books, 1959), 268. Reference here is to Hughes's notable poem, "Harlem" ("What Happens to a Dream Deferred?").

2. Blanche Radford-Curry, "Mothers Confronting Racism: Transforming the Lives of Our Children and Others," in *Everyday Acts against Racism: Raising Children in a Multiracial World* (Seattle: Seal Press, 1996), 132–43.

3. Norm Stamper, *Breaking Rank* (New York: Nation Books, 2005).

4. http://www.racismreview:com/blog/authopr/dr-tommy-j-curry/.

5. http://opinionator.blogs.nytimes.com/2015/01/12/whats-wrong-with-all-lives-matter/?_r=0.

6. Radford-Curry, "Mothers Confronting Racism," 140.

7. Associated with principles of Baha'i Faith, in particular "Oneness of Mankind [Humanity]," http://www.bahai.com/Bahaullah/principles.htm.

8. Martha Roth, "You Have to Start Somewhere," in *Everyday Acts against Racism: Raising Children in a Multiracial World* (Seattle: Seal Press, 1996), 3–11.

9. Shawn R. Donaldson, "When Our Faces Are at the Bottom of the Well," in *Everyday Acts against Racism: Raising Children in a Multiracial World* (Seattle: Seal Press, 1996), 99–109.

10. Donaldson, "When Our Faces Are at the Bottom of the Well," 100.

11. Derrick Bell, *Faces at the Bottom of the Well: The Permanence of Racism* (New York: Basic Books, 1992), 14.

12. Donaldson, "When Our Faces Are at the Bottom of the Well," 108.

13. *Post Traumatic Disorder*, Joy De Gruy Leary, YouTube,http://www.youtube.com/watch?v=XRQ-Ci6LwVw (accessed February 11, 2012).

14. Maya Angelou, *The Complete Collected Poems of Maya Angelou* (New York, Random House, 1994), "Phenomena Woman," 130–31.

15. Joy De Gruy Leary, http://www.youtube.com/watch?v=XRQ-Ci6LwVw (accessed February 11, 2012).

16. Bell, *Faces at the Bottom of the Well*, 14.

17. Donaldson, "When Our Faces Are at the Bottom of the Well," 101.

18. Bell, *Faces at the Bottom of the Well*, xi.

19. http://www.healingdoc.com/blogs/.

21. REGARDING HENRY

1. "Convicted Killer Speaks 50 Years after Slayings Which Inspired the Movie Mississippi Burning . . . but He STILL Won't Confess to Murdering Three Civil Rights Workers," *The Daily Mail*, December 22, 2014 (accessed December 29, 2014). http://www.dailymail.co.uk/news/article-2883979/Convict-1964-civil-rights-deaths-wont-confess.html.

2. "James Stern Invites Government to Investigate Klansman Edgar Ray Killen's Mississippi Property," *Huffington Post*, June 27, 2012, http://www.

huffingtonpost.com/2012/06/26/james-stern-invites-gover_n_1628611.html
(accessed January 14, 2015).

3. "James Stern Invites Government," *Huffington Post*.

4. "Three Civil Rights Activists Found Dead," BBC News, August 4, 1964,
http://news.bbc.co.uk/onthisday/hi/dates/stories/august/4/newsid_2962000/
2962638.stm (accessed December 29, 2014).

5. Here I borrow the title from Toni Morrison's Tanner Lecture on Human Values, "Unspeakable Things Unspoken: The Afro-American Presence in American Literature," University of Michigan, October 7, 1988.

6. Despite the twenty-year age gap between my father and uncle, my grandmother and grandfather transferred Henry's paternity to him for the sake of appearances and to continue to cover the illegitimacy and rape. Henry, though, knew the story of his father and had passed it on to his ex-wife. We later discovered that Henry had become addicted to heroin during his tours with the USO. My grandmothers were concerned about having a thirty-something-year-old drug addict in the home with four impressionable children—one of whom was a girl. There was very little understanding of and treatment for drug addiction in the late 1950s and early 1960s. My grandmother's mourning, though, is markedly similar to contemporary black mothers' mourning as a result of loss due to racist violence. Henry's difference due to the circumstances of his birth marked him, despite the fact that my grandmothers never treated him differently from the other children and grandchildren. The violence of his whiteness created for him a breach, and when he faltered, he and my grandmothers attributed it to the taint of white supremacy (in effect, the violence of whiteness). For my grandmothers, who were themselves clearly racially ambiguous and understood the tangled histories laced with white violence of their own conceptions (my great-grandfather's being half Irish, for example), Henry's intrusive whiteness was current and proved, from their perspective, and despite their best efforts at overwhelming it with a black bourgeois ethic, destructive to himself, his mother, and his family.

7. Toni Morrison, *The Bluest Eye* (New York: Random House, 2007), 126.

27. DEAR WILLIAM

1. http://www.quickmeme.com/meme/3sxou7 (accessed May 16, 2015).

2. http://www.progressive.org/news/2014/12/5047/letter-my-nephew (accessed May 16, 2015).

3. "The Ethical Demands of Integration," in *A Testament of Hope: The Essential Writings and Speeches of Martin Luther King, Jr.*, edited by James M. Washington (HarperOne, 2003), 122.

31. A LETTER TO DR. KING

1. *This letter is my attempt to speak not only as a scholar but also as a mother about the fears I have for my own children today. This letter was part of a talk that I gave at the University of Oklahoma Health Science Center to commemorate Martin Luther King Jr. Day, which for me has become a day to reflect on how far this country has come and how far we still need to go. The violent deaths of Eric Garner, Luis Rodriquez, and other black and brown people show the fragility of black existence under white supremacy. As was the case with Luis Rodriquez, one can be watching a movie at a theater and an hour later be dead in the parking lot at the hands of the police. As a way of providing context for readers, below is the beginning of the talk that I gave.* "When I was asked to speak at this event, the topic for my talk came to me at once. I knew that this would be a perfect time to reflect on my feelings about Trayvon Martin, Jordan Bell, Michael Brown, Eric Garner, Tamir Rice, Renisha McBride and the loss of countless other black and brown lives as well as the 'I can't breathe movement' that has taken root across the country in response to the failure of many in our society to see black and brown life as valuable.

"What I had to figure out was how to get my message across. I've always enjoyed the epistolary tradition, that is, telling stories through letter writing. I am also committed to the idea that 'listening is an act of love.' ('Listening is an act of love' is the tagline for the NPR program *StoryCorps.*) When we write letters to one another, we read the other's words, but we are also seeing the world through their eyes. So, in the hope that you would come to see my experience of the world, I decided that I would write a letter to Dr. Martin Luther King, Jr. to convey to him on his holiday the current state of affairs of race relations in this country. This letter is perhaps reminiscent of the letter that he wrote back in 1963 as he sat in that jail in Birmingham, Alabama. And although I am not a prisoner in the legal sense today, I cannot deny the fact that a society built on anti-black racism, prejudice, and the denial of black agency is not itself a sort of prison. So here it is, my letter to Dr. King."

2. Martin L. King Jr., "Letter from Birmingham City Jail," in *A Testament of Hope: The Essential Writings and Speeches of Martin Luther King Jr.*, edited by James M. Washington (New York: HarperSanFrancisco, 1986), 291.

3. King, "Letter."

4. Text excerpted from a poem in *Sing a Battle Song: Poems by Women in the Weather Underground Organization* (Brooklyn, NY: Weather Underground Organization, 1975).

5. https://www.whitehouse.gov/the-press-office/2013/01/21/inaugural-address-president-barack-obama (accessed August 2, 2015).

6. https://www.whitehouse.gov/the-press-office/2013/01/21/inaugural-address-president-barack-obama (accessed August 2, 2015).

32. A LETTER TO MY SONS

1. Margot Minardi, *Abolitionism and the Politics of Memory in Massachu-setts: Making Slavery History* (New York: Oxford University Press, 2010), 59.

2. Eric Porter, *The Problem of the Future World: W.E.B. Du Bois and the Race Concept at Midcentury* (Durham, NC: Duke University Press), 2010, 6.

RESOURCES

BOOKS:

Baldwin, James. *The Fire Next Time*. New York: Vintage, 1992.

Caldwell, Farai. *Black Lives Matter: A Collection of Short Stories*. Farai Art, 2015.

Camp, T. Jordan, and Heatherton, Christina. *Policing the Planet: Why the Policing Crisis Led to Black Lives Matter*. Brooklyn, NY: Verso, 2016.

Coates, Ta-Nehisi. *Between the World and Me*. New York: Spiegel & Grau, 2015.

Davis, Angela, and Barat, Frank. *Freedom Is a Constant Struggle: Ferguson, Palestine, and the Foundations of a Movement*. Chicago, IL: Haymarket Books, 2016.

Edwards, Sue Bradford, and Harris, Duchess. *Black Lives Matter*. Essential Library. 2015.

Golden, Maria. *Saving Our Sons*. New York: Anchor, 1995.

hooks, bell. *Happy to Be Nappy*. New York: Jump at the Sun, 1999.

Johnson, Charles, and Johnson, Elisheba. *Bending Time: The Adventures of Emery Jones*. Seattle, WA: Booktrope, 2013.

Lazarre, Jane. *Beyond the Whiteness of Whiteness: Memoir of a White Mother of Black Sons*. Durham, NC: Duke University Press, 2016.

Lester, Julius, and Barbour, Karen (illustrator). *Let's Talk About Race*. Augusta, KS: Amistad, 2008.

Taylor, Keeanga-Yamahtta. *From #BlackLivesMatter to Black Liberation*. Chicago, IL: Haymarket Books, 2016.

Ward, N.L. *I'm Just Saying: A Single Mother's Advice to a Son*. Seattle, WA: Amazon Digital Services LLC, 2016.

Wideman, John Edgar. *Fatheralong: A Meditation on Fathers and Sons, Race and Society*. New York: Vintage, 1995.

Yancy, George, and Hadley, Susan. *Therapeutic Uses of Rap and Hip Hop*. New York: Routledge, 2011.

Yancy, George, and Jones, Janine. *Trayvon Martin: Historical Contexts and Contemporary Manifestations of Racial Dynamics*. Lanham, MD: Lexington Books, 2014.

WEBSITES:

Black Moms Teach White Moms about Having "The Talk" with Their Sons: http://news.stlpublicradio.org/post/black-moms-teach-white-moms-about-having-talk-their-sons

Artist Honors the Black Mothers Who've Lost Their Sons to Police Brutality: http://www.huffingtonpost.com/entry/artist-honors-the-black-mothers-whove-lost-their-sons-to-police-brutality_us_572a4fa5e4b0bc9cb0458c69

Sylvia Maier, The Circle of Mothers Project: http://sylviamaier.com/circleofmothers/

Circle of Mothers. Trayvon Martin Foundation: http://london-alexander-nt2e.squarespace.com/circleofmothers/

Rankine, Claudia: http://mobile.nytimes.com/2015/06/22/magazine/the-condition-of-black-life-is-one-of-mourning.html?_r=1&referrer

Yancy, George: http://opinionator.blogs.nytimes.com/2013/09/01/walking-while-black-in-the-white-gaze/

Sister Song: http://sistersong.net/?option=com_content&view=article&id=25&Itemid=66

Trust Black Women: http://www.trustblackwomen.org

African American Policy Forum: http://www.aapf.org/kimberle-crenshaw/

Southerners on New Ground: http://southernersonnewground.org

National Organization of Parents of Murdered Children: http://www.pomc.com

The Counted: http://www.theguardian.com/us-news/ng-interactive/2015/jun/01/the-counted-police-killings-us-database

Say Her Name/Black Girls Matter: http://www.aapf.org/blackgirlsmatter/

Mothers of Black Sons: http://www.mobsmothers.org/

Black Mothers with Sons Organization: https://www.facebook.com/Black-Mothers-with-Sons-218751521487796/

INDEX

ABOUT THE CONTRIBUTORS

Jacki Lynn Baynks is a former facilitator with the Mother to Son Program offered by the nonprofit Small Seeds Development, Inc. in Pittsburgh. The Mother to Son Program (MTSP) is a unique model that offers single mothers and their African American sons ages eight to fifteen and siblings emotional support, education, a platform to share ideas, training, a safe environment, basic case management, as well as Council of Elders and mentoring. She has a bachelor of arts degree in English from Duquesne University and works full time for the University Writing Program of the University of North Carolina at Charlotte. She is the mother of two adult children and one grandson.

Shelly Bell, social entrepreneur, is among the nation's most sought-after writers, community organizers, and performers. Excelling as a truly dynamic force in the local (Washington, DC), national, and now international media, her work as a performance poet has led to an arts partnership with the Northern VA Fine Arts Association, an interview with NerdWallet, a performance with the world-renowned Washington Metro Philharmonic Association, and serving as an arts commissioner for the city of Alexandria, Virginia. Her organization, Women Writers Rock (WWR), exists to empower self-identified women to manifest radical messages into the world. WWR strives to create, support, and advocate for a community of women holding space to explore ideas and challenge societal norms. WWR envisions a world of safe people, safe spaces, and safe dwellings. The Teepee Project creates teepees to serve as safe dwelling spaces for self-identified women. Shelly was inspired to create Teepee BnB after hearing countless stories of the challenges that traveling women artists face when searching for a place to stay while on the road. The Teepees she creates are collapsible and can be stored when not in use. For more information on Shelly Bell visit http://www. iamshellybell.com.

Deborah Binkley-Jackson serves as director for the U.S. Department of Education TRIO program, Project Threshold—Student Support Services at the University of Oklahoma (OU). She holds a master's degree in human relations, and is currently a doctoral student in the OU Education Adult and Higher Learning program. Binkley-Jackson has several years of experience in home and community-based services and is certified as an Oklahoma Licensed Professional Counselor, and Behavioral Health Case Manager. She has served as president for the Oklahoma Division of Student Assistance programs (ODSA), and as president for the Oklahoma Association of Multicultural Counseling & Development, and maintains numerous board appointments and professional affiliations. Married to Norman police captain Ricky Jackson, they are the proud parents of two children, Lauren, an OU graduate, and Cameron, a sophomore at Southeastern Oklahoma State University.

Meta G. Carstarphen is professor at the University of Oklahoma in the Gaylord College of Journalism and Communication. A former associate dean and graduate director, Carstarphen has developed and taught classes in race/gender/class and the media, public relations, writing, and rhetoric. An award-winning feature writer, her books include *Sexual Rhetoric: Media Perspectives on Sexuality, Gender and Identity* (1999 and 2004), *Writing PR: A Multimedia Approach* (2011), *American Indians and the Mass Media*, and *Race, Gender Class and the Media*, second edition (2012).

Maria del Guadalupe Davidson is director of the Women's and Gender Studies Program and co-director of the Center for Social Justice at the University of Oklahoma. Her research areas include: rhetorical theory and criticism, the intersection of race and gender, black feminism, and Africana philosophical thought. Her new book, *Black Women, Agency, and the New Black Feminism*, is forthcoming. Dr. Davidson's most recent publications include the coedited volume *Exploring Race* *in Predominately White Classrooms: Scholars of Color Reflect* (with George Yancy). Dr. Davidson is currently working on a project about black women and curriculum design, and a large project that explores the one hundred-year anniversary of women's suffrage (1920–2020).

LaMar Delandro is a surveillance agent at the San Pablo Lytton Casino, and was a former Americorp Regional Supervisor in Richmond, California. He is a heavy thinker, is devoted to community health, is looking forward to finishing his college degree, and currently resides in Pinole, California.

Gretchen Givens Generett is associate professor in the Department of Educational Foundations and Leadership in the School of Education at Duquesne University. Her scholarly publications and teaching demonstrate her passion for breaking down barriers to successfully teach diverse student populations, along with evaluating and developing tools for effectively serving students of color. Her professional journey includes writing and editing books and journals in the field of education. She is a graduate of Spelman College and the University of North Carolina at Chapel Hill. She began her academic career at Virginia Tech and has served on the faculties of Shimabara Agricultural High School in Shimabara, Nagasaki, Japan; George Mason University; and Robert Morris University.

Jane Anna Gordon teaches political science and Africana studies at the University of Connecticut. She is coauthor of *Of Divine Warning* (2006), author of *Why They Couldn't Wait* (2001) and *Creolizing Political Theory* (2014), and coeditor of *Not Only the Master's Tools* (2005), *A Companion to African-American Studies* (2006), and *Creolizing Rousseau* (2015). She is president of the Caribbean Philosophical Association.

Farah Jasmine Griffin is William B. Ransford Professor of English and Comparative Literature and African-American Studies at Columbia University. She received her BA from Harvard (1985) and her PhD from Yale (1992). Professor Griffin's major fields of interest are American and African American literature, music, history, and politics. The recipient of numerous honors and awards for her teaching and scholarship, in 2006–2007 Professor Griffin was a fellow at the New York Public Library Cullman Center for Scholars and Writers. She is the author of *Who Set You Flowin': The African American Migration Narrative* (1995), *If You Can't Be Free, Be a Mystery: In Search of Billie Holiday* (2001), and *Clawing At the Limits of Cool: Miles Davis, John Coltrane, and the Greatest Jazz Collaboration Ever* (2008). She is also the editor of *Beloved Sisters and Loving Friends: Letters from Addie Brown and Rebecca Primus* (1999), coeditor with Cheryl Fish of *Stranger in the Village: Two Centuries of African American Travel Writing* (1998), and coeditor with Brent Edwards and Robert O'Meally of *Uptown Conversations: The New Jazz Studies* (2004).

Susan Hadley, PhD, MT-BC, is professor of music therapy at Slippery Rock University, Pennsylvania. Her books include *Experiencing Race as a Music Therapist: Personal Narratives* (2013), *Feminist Perspectives in Music Therapy* (2006), and *Psychodynamic Music Therapy: Case Studies* (2003). She coedited *Therapeutic Uses of Rap and Hip Hop* (2012) and *Narrative Identities: Psychologists Engaged in Self-Construction* (2005) with George Yancy. She has published numerous articles, encyclopedic entries, and chapters and reviews in scholarly journals and academic books. Dr. Hadley serves on the editorial boards of several journals and is coeditor in chief of the online journal, *Voices: A World Forum for Music Therapy*.

Carol E. Henderson is the vice provost for diversity and professor of English and Black American Studies at the University of Delaware. She has written or edited four books on African American literature and culture and written numerous journal articles and book chapters, the most recent being her article "AKA: Sarah Baartman, The Hottentot Venus, and Black Women's Identity" (*Women's Studies*, 2014). She has written on Emmett Till, Trayvon Martin, and Black mothers and sons in "Through the Eyes of a Mother: Reflections on the Rites of Passage of Black Boyhood." She is currently at work on a book project, *Scripting Black Childhood: Family, Community, and Violence in American Cinema*.

Dawn Herd-Clark is associate professor of history and chair of the Department of History, Geography, Political Science, and Criminal Justice at Fort Valley State University in Fort Valley, Georgia. Her most recent publications include the introduction to *T. Thomas Fortune's "After War Times": An African American Childhood in Reconstruction Era Florida*, edited by Daniel Weinfeld (2014) and "Jane Deveaux and Savannah Secret Schools," in *Slavery and Freedom in Savannah*, edited by Daina Berry and Leslie Harris (2014). In the area of grantsmanship, Herd-Clark recently secured a Smithsonian Institute and Georgia Humanities Council Museum on Main Street grant entitled Home Town Teams: How Sports Shape America. Of Herd-Clark's various accomplishments, her proudest to date is that of mother to two sons, Deondri II and Donyae.

Elisheba Johnson works at the intersection between social practice artist and arts administrator. She is a multimedia artist and poet, and has dedicated her career in the arts to creating space for emerging and POC artists to create and showcase their work. She has a BFA from Cornish College of the Arts and was the owner of Faire Gallery Café, a multi-use art space that held art exhibitions, music shows, poetry readings, and creative gatherings. Since 2013, Johnson has been at the Seattle Office of Arts of Culture where she is a liaison for the Seattle Arts Commission and works on capacity-building initiatives. In 2014, she co-wrote and published *The Adventures of Emery Jones: Boy Science Wonder* with her father Charles Johnson. She is also a founding member of COLLECT, a monthly curated art tour to inspire a new generation of art collectors. Johnson is currently a member of the Americans for the Arts Emerging Leaders council. When Johnson is not visiting an art exhibition with her son, she is a parenting advocate and travel enthusiast and fancies herself an amateur sommelier.

Heather Johnson is associate professor of sociology at Lehigh University. Her scholarship focuses on the intergenerational perpetuation of race and class inequality in the contemporary United States. She regularly gives talks on her work, and is the author of several publications, including the book *The American Dream and the Power of Wealth* (2014). She lives on campus at Lehigh University, as a faculty residential fellow, with her family. Her husband, Braydon, is the founder and CEO of RVibe, an Internet technology company. They adopted their twin sons, Kyle and Owen, from Haiti in 2005. Their daughter, Meera, was born in 2008. They keep a popular family blog at Johnson-mccormick.com, which chronicles their "'never-a-dull-moment life'" as a progressive, dual-career, inter-racial, adoptive, travel-loving, foodie family of five.

Newtona (Tina) Johnson is professor of English, director of Women's and Gender Studies, and interim vice provost for academic affairs at Middle Tennessee State University. Her research activities focus primarily on issues related to women and gender, particularly in the fields of postcolonial and African diaspora literature and critical theory. She has authored scholarly essays that have been published in peer-reviewed journals such as *Research in African Literatures*, *Obsidian III: Literature of the African Diaspora*, *MaComère: Journal of the Association of Caribbean Women Writers and Scholars*, and *The CEA Critic*. She has also contributed scholarly essays to edited volumes. In addition, Johnson has made numerous presentations in her areas of research, particularly at international scholarly conferences. Johnson was one of fifty faculty and administrators across the United States selected as an American Council on Education (ACE) Fellow for 2013–2014.

Jane Lazarre is a prize-winning writer of fiction and nonfiction. Her most recent novels are *Inheritance* and *Some Place Quite Unknown*. Other works include, *The Powers of Charlotte*, and *Worlds Beyond My Control*, novels, and memoirs: *The Mother Knot*, *On Loving Men*, *Beyond the Whiteness of Whiteness: Memoir of a White Mother of Black Sons*, *Wet Earth*, and *Dreams: A Narrative of Grief and Recovery*. Her newly completed memoir, *The Communist and the Communist's Daughter*, will be published in the next year. Lazarre has taught writing and literature at the City College of New York, Yale University, and Eugene Lang College at the New School, where she created and directed the undergraduate writing program and served on the full-time faculty for twenty years. She serves on the board of directors of Brotherhood-SisterSol, an organization in Harlem serving children and youth and teaches writing privately. Please go to http://www.janelazarre.com for complete bio and history.

Sara Lomax-Reese is the president and general manager of WURD Radio, LLC, Pennsylvania's only African American–owned talk radio station. She hosted and produced the "HealthQuest Live" radio show on WURD from 2002 through 2013. Prior to her work with WURD, Sara cofounded *HealthQuest: Total Wellness for Body, Mind & Spirit*, the first nationally circulated African American consumer health magazine in the country. A graduate of the University of Pennsylvania and Columbia University Graduate School of Journalism, Sara also served as adjunct professor of communications at Oglethorpe University in Atlanta, Georgia. She has taught a collaborative course at the University of Pennsylvania with Dr. John Jackson, titled "Urban Ethnography," which taught students how to create audio documentaries that aired on 900AM-WURD. Sara has received numerous awards including: the Woman of Substance Award from the National Medical Association; the "Tree of Life" award from the Wellness of You; and *HealthQuest* magazine received the Beacon of Light Award from the Congressional Black Caucus for outstanding health coverage. Sara was recognized as one of the "100 People to Watch" by *Business Philadelphia* magazine, and in 2010, she was selected for the "Women of Distinction" award given by the *Philadelphia Business Journal*. Most recently, Sara received the 2012 PECO "Power to the Community" award given by the National Coalition of 100 Black Women of Pennsylvania. Sara sits on a variety of boards including the Kimmel Center for Performing Arts, Pennsylvania Academy of the Fine Arts, and the Maternity Care Coalition's Riverside Correctional Facility working group. She is married to Tim Reese and is the mother of three boys, Langston, Elijah, and Julian.

Tracey McCants Lewis JD, is assistant clinical law professor at Duquesne University School of Law. She is also the director of the pro bono program. She teaches in the Civil Rights and Unemployment Compensation Clinics, where she supervises students representing clients in employment discrimination matters and unemployment compensation hearings. She also supervises students who provide reentry legal assistance to individuals seeking expungements and/or governor's pardon. Her writings include "A Mother's Pain, the Toxicity of the Systemic Disease of Devaluation Transferred from Black Mother to Black Male Child," in *Pursuing Trayvon Martin: Historical Contexts and Contemporary Manifestations of Racial Dynamics* and "Legal Storytelling: The Murder of Voter ID" (2015). Most recently she gave a

TEDx Talk entitled "Activate Forgiveness—Eradicate the Box," about employment reentry barriers.

Nicole McJamerson works for the Department of Social Services. She has written and performed cultural criticism through live film narration at REDCAT (Los Angeles), the Velaslavasay Panorama (Los Angeles), the de Young Museum (San Francisco), and Artist's Television Access (San Francisco). She lives in California's Santa Clarita Valley with her family.

Michele Moody-Adams is Joseph Straus Professor of Political Philosophy and Legal Theory at Columbia University, where she also served as dean of Columbia College and vice president for undergraduate education. She has also taught at Cornell University, where she was vice provost for undergraduate education, Wellesley College, the University of Rochester, and Indiana University, where she served as associate dean. Moody-Adams is the author of *Fieldwork in Familiar Places: Morality, Culture and Philosophy* and has published numerous articles on equality and social justice, moral psychology and the virtues, and the philosophical implications of gender and race. Her recent publications include articles on academic freedom, equal educational opportunity, and democratic disagreement. She is writing a book, *Renewing Democracy*, on the political culture and institutions essential to achieving justice and promoting stability in multicultural democracies. She has a BA from Wellesley College, a second BA from Oxford University, and an MA and PhD in philosophy from Harvard University.

Elisha Oliver is a biocultural anthropologist. She is a veteran educator and has over fifteen years of teaching experience. Elisha has taught in public and private school settings as well as developed and taught anthropology courses for the University of Oklahoma and the Duke University TIP program. Elisha serves as an educational consultant and curriculum developer for a small nonprofit group in Oklahoma that serves talented and gifted students; and, through her co-owned research firm, Healthy Life Course Research Center, Elisha conducts community-based participatory maternal- and child-health research. Currently, Elisha is working on an ethnographic documentary about identity and intersectionality.

Blanche Radford-Curry is professor of philosophy and College of Arts and Sciences assistant dean at Fayetteville State University, Fayetteville, North Carolina. She received her PhD in philosophy from Brown University. She has published in *SAGE: A Scholarly Journal on Black Women, Educational Foundations,* and the *American Philosophical Association Newsletter on Philosophy and the Black Experience.* She has also contributed chapters in *Overcoming Racism and Sexism, Gender and Academe: Feminist Pedagogy and Politics, Women's Studies in Transition: The Pursuit of Interdisciplinarity,* and *What White Looks Like: African-American Philosophers on the Whiteness Question.* Her areas of research include African American Philosophy, Multicultural Theory, and Feminist Theory.

Autumn Redcross is a PhD student in the Department of Communication & Rhetorical studies at Duquesne University. As an active volunteer in her community committed to creating forums to facilitate responsible conversations about race, she founded the annual Juneteenth celebration in Sewickley and coauthored an Arcadia Images in America book, *African Americans in Sewickley Valley.* Her current research interests include notions of black capital, *black body memory,* the rhetoric of applied anthropology, and critical race philosophy.

Tracey Reed Armant is a program associate with the Grable Foundation. The Grable Foundation is guided by the mission to help children and youth become independent, caring, contributing members of society, by supporting programs critical to a child's successful development. Tracey has a PhD in educational policy from the University of Virginia and has dedicated her professional life to improving life chances for children. Tracey lives in Pittsburgh with her husband and two children.

Noliwe Rooks is associate professor in Africana studies at Cornell University where she is also the director of graduate studies in Africana studies. She is the author of three books: *Hair Raising: Beauty, Culture and African American Women* (which won both the 1997 Choice Award for Outstanding Academic Book and the Public Library Association's 1997 award for Outstanding University Press Book); *Ladies Pages: African American Women's Magazines and the Culture That Made*

Them; and *White Money/Black Power: African American Studies and the Crises of Race in Higher Education*.

T. Denean Sharpley-Whiting is the Gertrude Conaway Vanderbilt Distinguished Professor of African American and Diaspora Studies and French at Vanderbilt University where she also directs the Callie House Research Center for the Study of Global Black Cultures and Politics. She is senior coeditor of the journal *Palimpsest* and coeditor of the Blacks and Diaspora series and Philosophy and Race series. Her latest books include: *Bricktop's Paris: African American Women in Paris between the Two World Wars* and *The Autobiography of Ada Bricktop Smith, or Miss Baker Regrets* (2015) and the academic murder mystery *The 13th Fellow: A Mystery in Provence* (2015).

Treasure Shields Redmond, a native of Mississippi, is a St. Louis metro-based poet, performer, and social justice educator. She most recently featured at the Nuyorican Poets Café. She has published poetry in such notable anthologies as *Bum Rush the Page: A Def Poetry Jam*, *Breaking Ground: A Reader Celebrating Cane Canem's First Decade* and in journals that include *The Sou'wester* and the *African American Review*. Treasure has received a fellowship to the Fine Arts Works Center, and her poem, "around the time of medgar" was nominated for a 2011 Pushcart Prize. Her collection titled *chop: 30 kwansabas for fannie lou hamer* will be published in the fall of 2015. A Cave Canem fellow, who has received an MFA from the University of Memphis, Treasure divides her time between being assistant professor of English at Southwestern Illinois College and doctoral studies at Indiana University of Pennsylvania.

Regina Sims Wright is associate professor in the School of Nursing at the University of Delaware. She earned her PhD from the Department of Psychology at Howard University in 2007. Dr. Wright's research examines the association between cardiovascular disease risk factors and cognitive function among older adults. Much of this work focuses on the disparate health and cognitive outcomes experienced by African American older adults. She has published widely in peer-reviewed gerontological, medical, and psychological journals. She currently serves on the board of trustees of the Wilmington Senior Center, a predominately African American senior center in Wilmington, Delaware.

Sharyn Skeeter was fiction/poetry/book review editor at *Essence* and editor in chief of *Black Elegance*. During her time at *Essence*, she was a judge of the United Negro College Fund's poetry competition. Her poetry has been published in various literary journals and anthologies, including *Poet Lore*, *In Search of Color Everywhere* (edited by E. Ethelbert Miller), *The Cafe Review*, *Re-Markings*, and *Charles Johnson: Embracing the World*. She has taught at Emerson College, the University of Bridgeport, Fairfield University, and Gateway Community College. She is working on a novel and a collection of poetry.

Becky Thompson, poet, activist, scholar, yogi, is the author of several books on social justice including, *Mothering without a Compass: White Mother's Love, Black Son's Courage, Survivors on the Yoga Mat: Stories for Those Healing from Trauma*, and *A Promise and a Way of Life: White Antiracist Activism*. Becky is chair of the Sociology Department at Simmons College, teaches yoga at the Dorchester YMCA in Boston, and lives with her daughter in Jamaica Plain, Massachusetts.

Linda D. Tomlinson is tenured associate professor of history and undergraduate program coordinator for the Department of Government and History at Fayetteville State University in Fayetteville, North Carolina. Tomlinson is an Americanist with a focus on African American history. Her research and writing include the Civil Rights and Black Power movements, Black grassroots activism, African American women's activism, and cultural transformations in the African diaspora. She holds a BA in Communication Arts/Public Relations and MLA in history from Southern Methodist University (SMU) in Dallas, Texas. In addition, she holds a doctorate degree in African and African American studies (AAAS) from Clark Atlanta University in Atlanta, Georgia. She is married and currently lives in Fayetteville, North Carolina.

Dyan Watson is associate professor of education at the Lewis & Clark Graduate School of Education and Counseling in Portland, Oregon, and serves as the social studies coordinator for the secondary program in teacher education. She teaches methods classes for preservice social studies teachers and research methods classes for doctoral students and researches how race mediates teaching. She is also an editor for *Rethinking Schools*. Some of her publications include "Letter from a Black Mom to her Son," "'Urban, but Not Too Urban': Unpacking Teachers' Desires to Teach Urban Students," and "Norming Suburban: How Teachers Talk about Race without Using Race Words." She is also the coeditor of *Rhythm and Resistance: Teaching Poetry for Social Justice* and *Rethinking Elementary Education*. She is the mother of two black sons.

Veronica T. Watson is professor of English at Indiana University of Pennsylvania in the Graduate Program in Literature and Criticism. She is coeditor of *Unveiling Whiteness in the 21st Century: Global Manifestations, Transdisciplinary Interventions* (2015) and author of *The Souls of White Folk: African American Writers Theorize Whiteness* (2013). Her work has appeared in a number of collections and academic journals, including *African American Review, Mississippi Quarterly*, and *The Journal of Ethnic American Literature*. She is convener of the Frederick Douglass Institute Collaborative of Pennsylvania's State System of Higher Education.

Karsonya Wise Whitehead is author of several book chapters, articles, and opinion editorials, and four books, *RaceBrave: New and Selected Works* (2016), *Letters to My Black Sons: Raising Boys in a Post-Racial? America* (2015), *Notes from a Colored Girl: The Civil War Pocket Diaries of Emilie Frances Davis* (2014), and *Sparking the Genius: The Carter G. Woodson Lecture* (2014) and coeditor of *Coleman: His Art Story* (2016) and *Rethinking Emilie Frances Davis: Lesson Plans for Teaching Her 1863–1865 Pocket Diaries* (2014). Her forthcoming book, *The Emancipation Proclamation: Race Relations on the Eve of Reconstruction*, is due out in 2017.

George Yancy is professor of philosophy at Emory University. He received his BA (with honors) in philosophy from the University of Pittsburgh, his first master's degree from Yale University in philosophy, and his second master's degree in Africana Studies from New York University, where he received a distinguished fellowship. His PhD (with distinction) is in philosophy from Duquesne University. His work focuses primarily in the areas of critical philosophy of race, critical whiteness studies, and philosophy of the black experience. He has authored, edited, or coedited over seventeen books and many academic articles and book chapters. Yancy's work has been cited as far away as South Africa, Australia, Turkey, and Sweden. His first authored book received an honorable mention from the Gustavus Myers Center for the Study of Bigotry and Human Rights and three of his edited books have received *CHOICE* outstanding academic book awards. He is editor of the Philosophy of Race book series at Lexington Books, and is known for his interviews and articles on the subject of race at The Stone forum of the *New York Times*.